Book Cover

Design Wizardry

For the Self-Publishing Author

Timothy Fish

Comments? Questions?

If at any time you wish to make a comment concerning this book, please feel free to e-mail the author at:

bookcomments@timothyfish.net

You may also like to visit the author's blog:

http://timothyfish.blogspot.com

On his blog, Timothy frequently covers writing topics and other things.

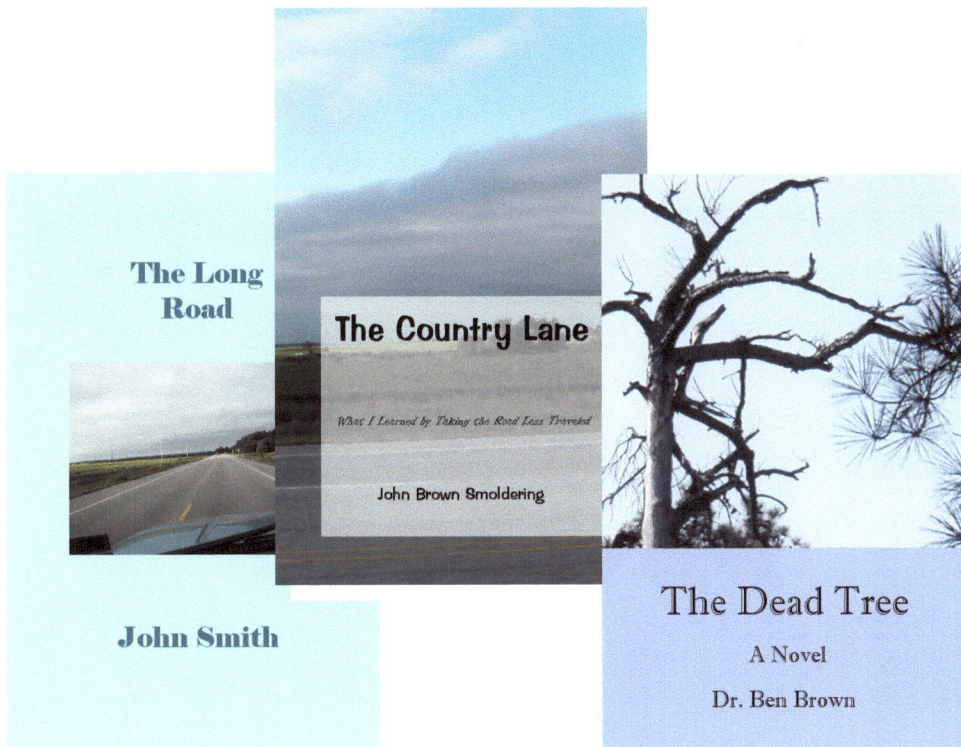

The Curse of the Bad Covers

I know you've seen them. They're everywhere. A friend tells you about his latest book and you've got to take a look, but what you find is a book with a generic cover that looks very similar to the covers you see above. Maybe you aren't even sure why it is so obvious, but the cover screams at you: Cheap book! Self-published!

And it might not be self-published at all. Whether it is or it isn't, it may not deserve to be called a cheap book, but how can you tell? We've always been told not to judge a book by its cover, but we do. We see a cover like the covers seen here and we make some assumptions about the book. In many cases they are well founded. Traditional publishers that use a cheap cover design may do so because they lack confidence that the book will sell many copies. It takes time to produce a better looking cover and time is money. Subsidy presses also try to cut costs by using generic covers for the same reason.

Wherever they come from, you don't want a generic on your book. It's possible that you already have such a book. Though it may not prevent you from selling books, a generic cover doesn't do anything to help. The cover is forgettable. Someone will look at your cover and think he's seen it before and he probably has.

One of the sources for generic covers is through cover generating software that subsidy presses and self-publishing companies make available to their customers. The nice thing about software like this is that in a matter of minutes you can have a cover that fits your book perfectly. But your choices are somewhat limited. Sure, you may have thirty or so templates available and a couple thousand stock images you can use, but templates are designed to be generic. They are designed in such a way that any of the thousands of photos available to you will fit in the photo areas. They are designed in such a way that the text won't interfere with the graphics. Because they have to work for so many different people with so many different books, they tend to get a common feel to them.

The purpose of the book you are reading is to give you the tools you need to avoid the curse of the generic covers. But it won't be easy. Bad covers are easy to design. The cover on the right took about five minutes to design and save to a file format suitable for Publish On Demand (POD) printing. It would have taken slight longer to include the spine and back cover, but it doesn't take long to slap in a picture, a rectangle for text and the text on the cover. Good covers, on the other hand, can take several hours to complete and if you are paying someone to do the work can cost hundreds of dollars. If you're willing to put in the time, you can produce a cover that doesn't look like a cheap cover and won't cost you a lot of money either. If you aren't, you might as well put this book down now and find something else to do with your time. But if you're willing, it can be enjoyable and you can have a cover you are proud of.

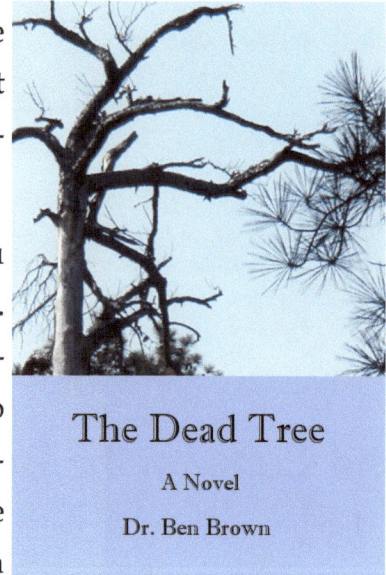

For the Common Man

I almost called this book *Cover Design for the Common Man* after Aaron Copland's *Fanfare for the Common Man*. If you're wondering how it applies, let me point out that profession book cover designers often go to school to learn their trade. They take art classes where they learn about the golden rectangle and the rule of thirds and all kinds of other fun stuff. They learn to use tools like Photoshop. Many of them may be faithful Mac users. But us. Most authors use Windows and find the $650 price tag on the full version of Pho-

2

toshop a little steep. While we may find ourselves in the position of being forced to design our own cover, we don't have the benefit of years of experience in the visual arts. So what you should expect from this book is that you'll be able to accomplish all you need to accomplish without spending hundreds of dollars on software or going down to your community college to learn how to use Photoshop. In fact, the software you'll need to work through the examples in this book is free. Our tools of choice will be The Gimp (more commonly called Gimp) and Inkscape. These are both available to download at the following addresses:

http://www.gimp.org/windows/

http://inkscape.org/download/

For those of you who have never seen these programs before, The Gimp is an open source software package that is similar to Photoshop. If you already own Photoshop, it shouldn't be difficult to transfer the techniques described here to Photoshop, since they have similar capabilities, but you will see some differences in the user interface. Inkscape is a vector graphics tool that is similar to Adobe Illustrator, Corel Draw, Freehand, and Xara X.

The Gimp is a roster graphics tool. The concept behind it is that it sets the value of each pixel in an image. For many purposes, that is exactly what we want, but we run into problems when we decide to scale an image. Once we increase the size of the image, it will either become pixelated or blurry. This is where a tool like Inkscape can be particularly useful. The images that are drawn in vector graphics scale nicely. Since the book printing process looks for image resolutions of 300 pixels per inch or even more, the scalability of vector graphics is very useful. However, there are some things that are difficult to represent with vector graphics. For that reason, we will use each tool for different purposes.

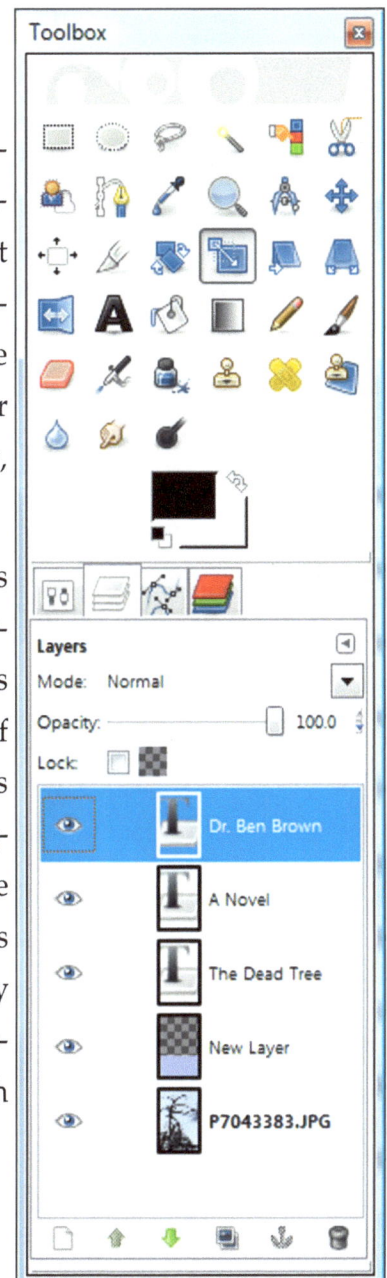

An Introduction to The Gimp

Once you get The Gimp installed, one of the best thing you can do is to play with it for a few minutes to get used to the interface. Several of the tools are self-explanatory. A selection tool is a selection tool. A paint brush is a paint brush. We'll be using The Gimp a lot and if you aren't already used to it, you'll get used to the interface as we go along. You'll find that we'll use the layers frequently as well as the tool tab. There is also a paths tab that we'll be using.

If at any time you see a table here that you don't see on your own machine, left click the backward facing arrow shown here and select "Add Tab". You will need to add the "Paths" tab for some of what we'll be doing.

Don't let Gimp overwhelm you. Once you get used to it, you'll see that it is a very powerful tool with a relatively simple user interface.

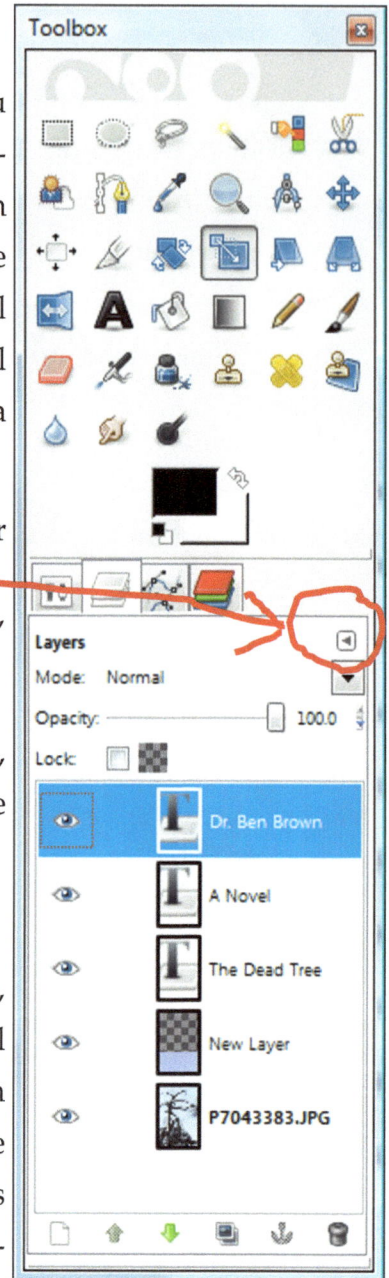

The Simplest Cover

Book Title

Before we begin designing a book cover, we need to be comfortable with our tool of choice. One way to do that is to design the most simple of all covers. Once we have done that, many of the techniques we use can be repeated on more complicated covers. The cover we will design

Joe Q. Author

will have black text on a white background with a title and an author's name. In other words, it will look like a book would look if it had no cover at all. It might look very much like the cover that you see here. It doesn't look complicated and yet there is much you can learn by designing a cover like this, beginning creating a template.

Creating a Template

Often the company you are using to publish your book will provide you with a tem-

4

plate that will tell you where to place the text and graphics for your cover. CreateSpace has a template builder that is located at https://www.createspace.com/Products/Book/#content4 that can be used to create the covers for many books. If you spend some time playing with it, you'll see that their tool will generate a zip file that has files that we can use as one of the layers in Gimp. As we work, we can turn that layer on or off, allowing us to do our work. But you don't have to use their template and sometimes the templates are not available. Ironically, there was not a template for the book you hold in your hand. To handle that possibility, we will build our own here. It will also serve as a demonstration of some of the techniques needed to do other things.

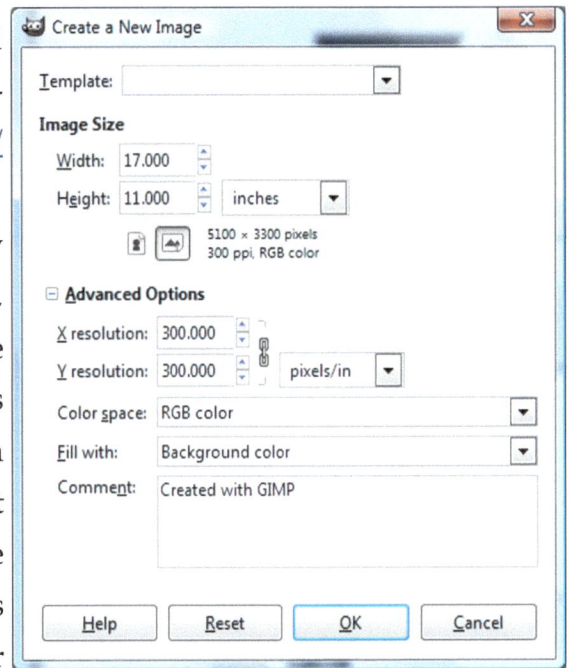

Create a New Image

To create a new image select File|New… and Gimp will bring up the dialog box shown above. You will need to expand the Advanced Options and then make the selections that are required to make your new image match this one.

Notice that we are using a width of 17 inches, a height of 11 inches and the resolution is 300 pixels per inch. The company you are working with may ask you to use different values, but this are the values I would expect to see at most companies. The printing process is not very forgiving of low resolution images, so a resolution of at least 300 is needed. The width and height are of a standard sized piece of paper. If you are using POD printing, they will be printing the cover on a sheet that size and then trimming it to match the book.

You may get a warning about the size of the image. Click Ok.

This will produce a very large image with a white background. Use the view scaler that is circled in the image below to set the size of the screen to a

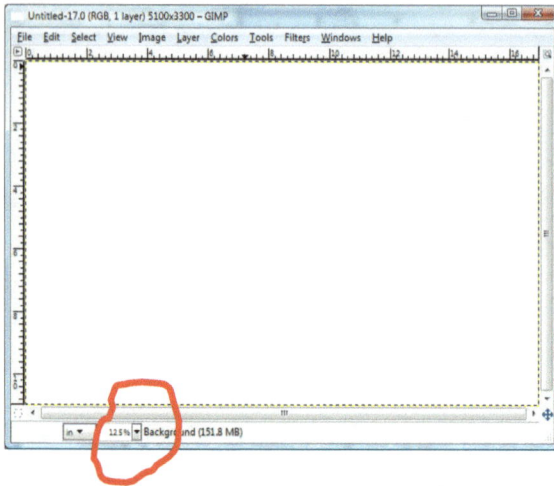

more manageable size. It is unlikely that you screen will be large enough to hold the whole image without scaling it down.

You can usually work on the image while it is scaled down to a lower size, so as we manipulate the image you will be working with it at a resolution we're more familiar working with on the computer, but we may need to push the scaling up in order to see what we've been doing.

Create a New Layer

We first created a very large image. All it is now is a white background. For our template, we need a transparent layer. We create this layer by clicking the new layer button at the bottom of the Toolbox window. This will bring up a dialog box like the one show below. Set the Layer name to "Template" or whatever name you would like to use to identify this layer and set the rest of the values to the same values shown here. This will create a layer that is transparent. We will be able to edit this layer without messing up any of the other layers. Our background will remain white. We will show the template when we need it and hide it at other times.

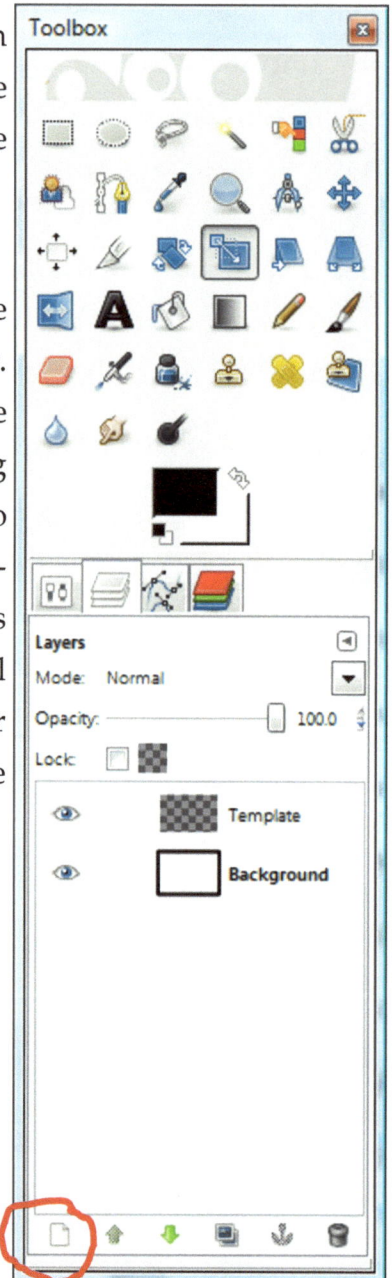

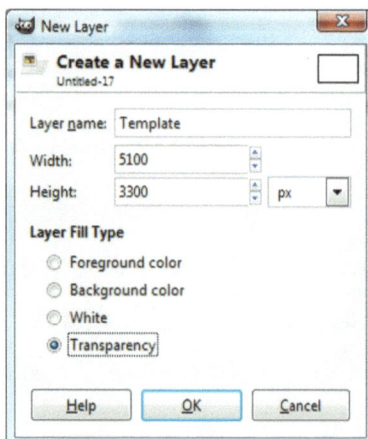

Draw the Boundaries

Unlike the simple front cover we saw at the beginning of this section, a cover is not simply a title in a rectangular box. For a paperback book, we have three separate areas to work with, the front, the back, and the spine. The concept is simple, but we must get these areas positioned exactly or the knife that trims the edges of the book may slice through the text on the cover or the spine of the book may appear on the fold.

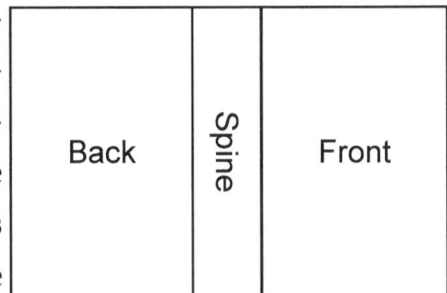

While Gimp does allow you to define guides, Gimp's guides will not work well for our purposes. Instead, we will draw selection boxes, position them in the right places, convert them to paths, and draw borders around the paths. But first, we have to determine the size of each area and where they need to be positioned. There is some simple math involved in determining where these areas should be located on the 17"x11" page.

In this book, we will always use book dimensions that are 6"x9" because this is a commonly used size for POD books, but you can use whatever size you need. The dimension we don't know at this point is the height of the book, which is the width of the spine. That value is determined by the number of pages in the book and the thickness of the paper. We can't use a ruler to measure the thickness of a sheet of paper, so we first have to get that information from the company that will be printing the book. It can make a difference between white paper, cream paper, and the paper used for full color printing. The book you hold in your hand has a page multiplier of 0.002347. So, if you were to use the same paper for a 200 page book, the book would be 0.002347×200 or 0.4694 inches. Because we are working with 300 pixels per inch, that is also 141 pixels.

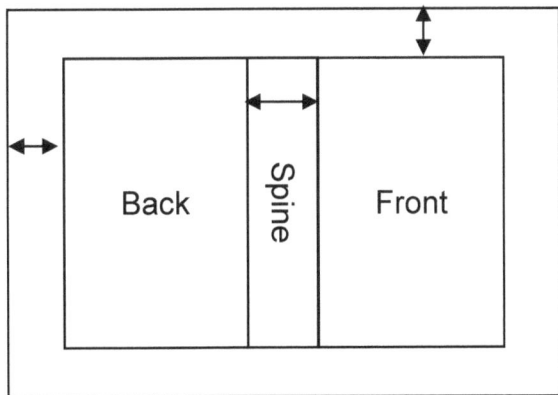

By adding the widths of the front and back covers to the size of the spine, we find that the book cover is 12.4694 inches from edge to edge. We center this on the 17"x11" page by subtracting 12.4694 from 17 and dividing by 2. (17 - 12.4694) = 4.5306. 4.5306/2 = 2.2653, giving us the distance of the edge of the back cover to the edge of our drawing area. We do the same with the other dimension giving us, (11-9)/2 = 1 and we can begin to draw this area on our Template layer in Gimp.

Choose the Rectangular Section tool from the toolbox.

With the Template layer choose, draw a selection box anywhere in the drawing area. It doesn't have to be exact because we will use the Selection Tool's options to reposition it correctly.

Switch to the Tool Options tab.

Select the area needed for the back cover by modifying the selection options to look like the image show here:

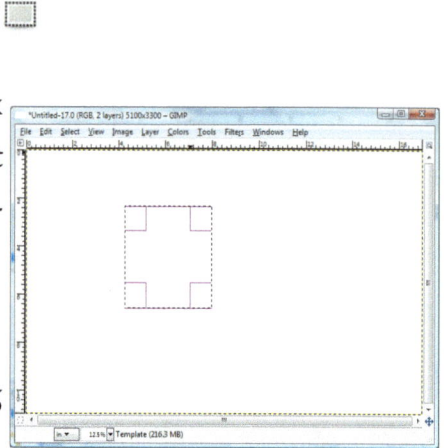

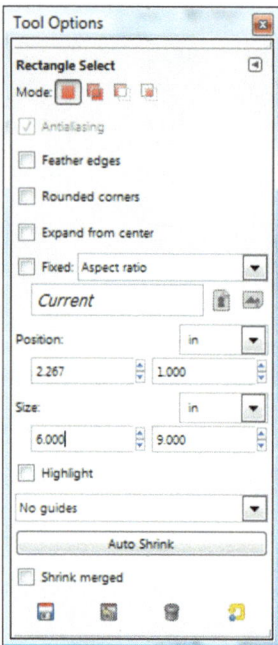

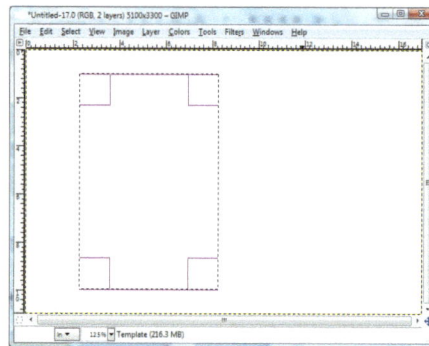

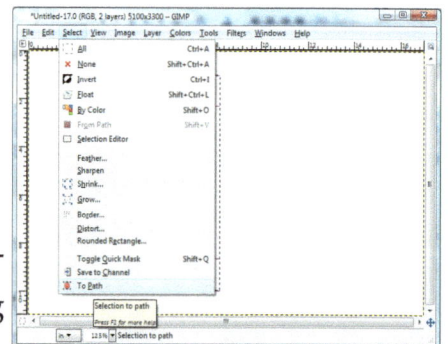

Now, convert the selection into a Path by from the Select menu. The new Path will appear in the Paths dialog window. Which is available from Windows|Dockable Dialogs|Paths.

Right click on the path in the Paths dialog and change the name to "Back" so that you will recognize it later.

8

Right click again and choose the Stroke Path menu item. The default settings should be adequate. It will give us a rectangle drawn in whatever color we've selected.

Repeat this process for the Spine and the Front, with the exception that their dimensions and placement should be as is shown below:

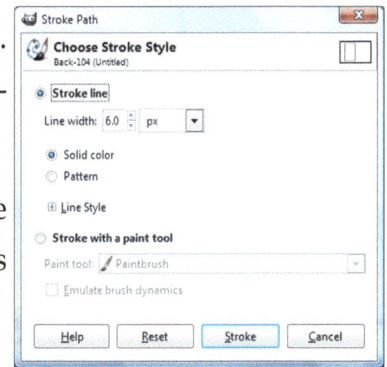

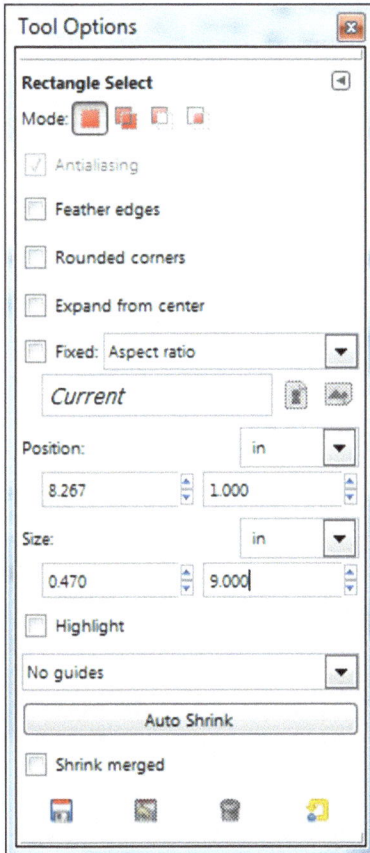

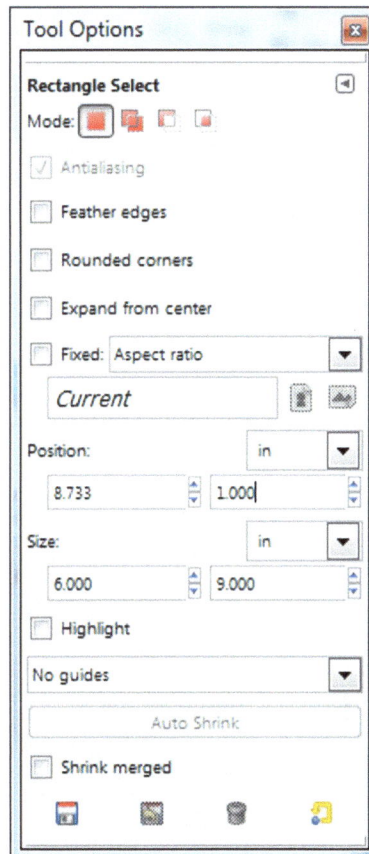

After you have completed all of that, you should have something that looks like this. If you click the eye beside the Template layer, the lines should all disappear, leaving you with a white screen again. With the lines visible, you will be able to see where you can place you text and graphics on the other layers. But we need to add one more

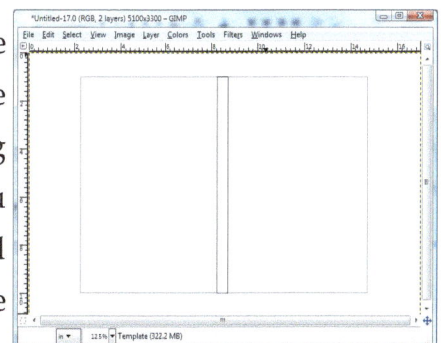

thing so we can protect ourselves from getting too close to the edge.

Because of the way books are printed and trimmed, the knife may cut at a slightly different place than we planned. Just the variation in the thickness of paper can have an impact. We need to avoid placing live text and graphics within the area that is about 0.25" inside the edge of the cover. We also need to allow for at least 0.125" on the outside of the cover for the bleed area. Any images that we want to extend to the edge of the book should extend all the way through that 0.125" margin so that the knife has enough to slice through. You will see examples of that later in this book. For now, we just need to mark these areas on our template.

Select all of the area for the book cover by right clicking each of the paths in the Path Dialog in turn and selecting Add to Selection. The ants should be walking along the edge of the cover.

Choose Select|Grow and enter a value of 0.125 inches, as is shown here.

Next, right click on the paths in turn again, but this time select Subtract from Selection.

Now, the only thing selected should be a border outside of the cover lines.

Select the Template Layer to make it active then, change the primary color to Red.

Using the Paint Bucket Fill tool. Fill the selection with Red.

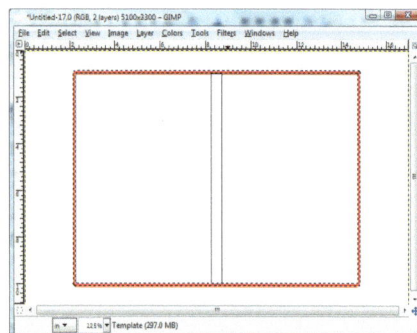

The technique for drawing the interior area is similar.

From the Select menu, choose Select None to get us back to a known state.

As before, select the area of the book cover by right clicking each of the paths in turn and choosing Add to Selection.

This time, choose Select|Shrink… from the menu and enter a value of 0.25 inches.

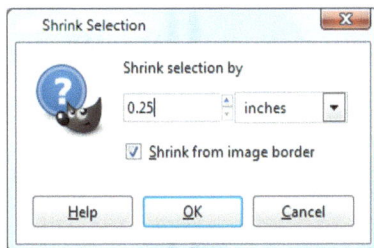

This will give us a selection of the Safe area of our template, but we want to draw a line in the unsafe area. So invert the selection by choosing Select|Invert.

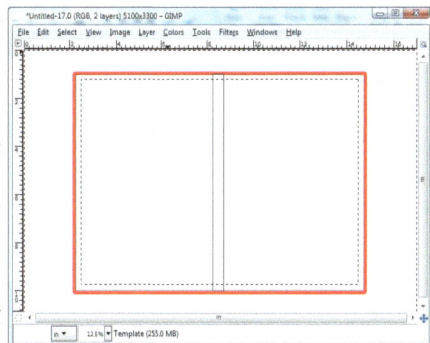

You won't see much difference except that the ants are now running along the outside of the drawing area as well as in the previously selected area.

Select the Template Layer to make it active and select the Color Yellow.

Using the Paint Bucket Fill tool set to Fill Similar Colors, click on the interior areas between the red line and the dancing ants. This will produce the result seen here.

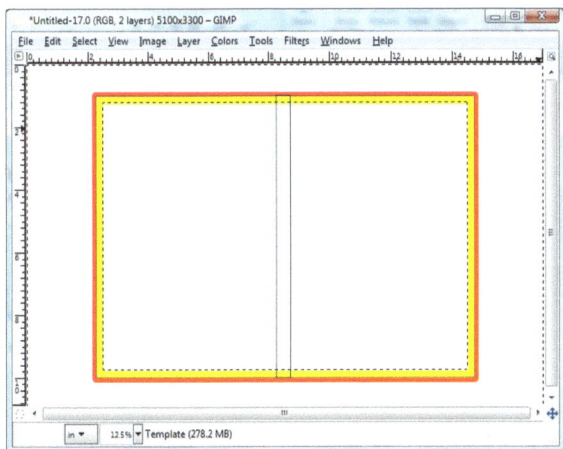

Keeping in mind that you may need to leave space for the barcode near the bottom of the back cover, this is the basics of a template. Save your work, first as a .xcf file, which is the Gimp file format. Then hide the background layer by clicking the eye and save the file as a .png file. I called mine *Template.png* and you will be seeing it again several times throughout this book.

Calculating Dimensions

Spine Width:

[Number of Pages] × [Page Multiplier Specified by Printer]

Edge to Edge Cover Size:

([Book Width] × 2) + [Spine Width]

Distance from Top of Drawing Area to Cover Top Edge:

(11 - [Book Length]) / 2

Distance from Left of Drawing Area to Back Left Edge:

((17 - [Spine Width]) / 2) - [Book Width]

Distance from Left to Spine Left Edge:

(17 - [Spine Width]) / 2

Distance from Left to Front Left Edge:

(17 + [Spine Width]) / 2

Distance from Left to Back Center:

(17 - [Spine Width] - [Book Width]) / 2

Distance from Left to Spine Center:

17 / 2

Distance from Left to Front Center:

(17 + [Spine Width] + [Book Width]) / 2

Note: These assume that the cover will be printed on a 17x11 inch sheet of paper. If that is not true for you, simply replace 17 and 11 with the respective dimensions.

Back to Creating the Simplest Cover

With a template to tell us where we can place things, creating the simple cover is really just as easy as positioning the text where we need it.

Gimp has a text tool for us to use **A** .

Select the tool and draw a box that stretches across the front cover area of the drawing.

Notice that when I made my selection I included the yellow line on the right side of the cover. Even though we don't want our text to go into that area, we want Gimp to include it when it calculates the midpoint for the text. If it doesn't the end result will be a cover with the text shifted to the left. The appearance will be that of a book that doesn't have enough trimmed from the right side.

Replicate what I have done here. You can reposition your text to wherever you want it and can select whatever font you want. Repeat the process to place the author's name on the front cover.

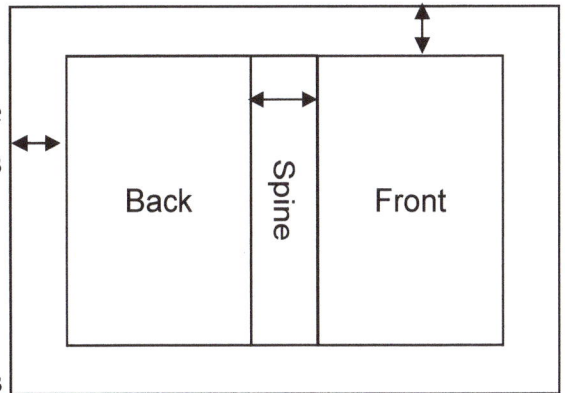

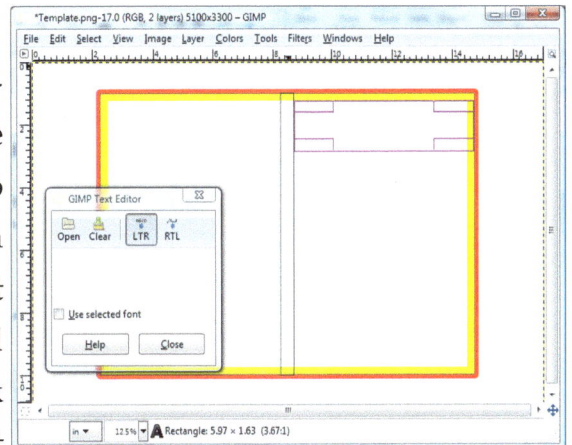

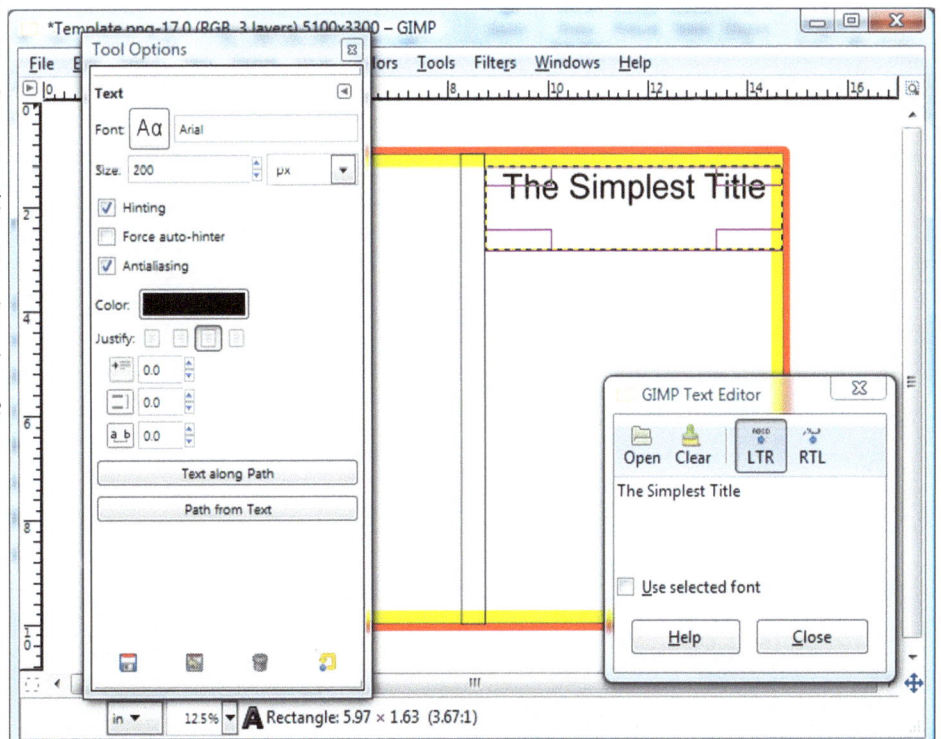

We run into a slight problem when we attempt to add lettering to the spine. Gimp is sophisticated enough that when we use the text tool it will create a text layer for the text and we can go back later to edit the text, change the font, change the size, etc. Unfortunately, when we choose to rotate the text, Gimp converts the text into pixel data and our ability to modify the text is hampered.

This text is a text layer.

This text is pixels.

Note that Gimp does have some ability to keep up with the fact that the text that has been converted to pixels was once text and clicking on it with the text tool will bring up a dialog box asking if we want to undo the non-text changes so we can edit the text.

We have a few options. We can either deal with Gimp's limitations and move on or we can move our image into a tool that gives us better text tools. Inkscape, which I mentioned before, is much more user friendly when it comes to manipulating text. Or you might want to move your graphic into a desktop publishing program of some kind. I have often done all but the text in Gimp or another tool and then moved over into Microsoft Publisher because Publisher was easier to use for text. But if you need to use Gimps tools for adding shadows and the like to text, it is often easier to just work around the limitations, as we will do for our simple cover.

Use the Text Tool **A** again to create the text. Set the font size to an appropriate size. I used 100 point Arial.

Use the Rotate Tool ⟱ to rotate the text. Rather than using the mouse, enter 90 degrees into the Rotate Tool dialog box. Then reposition the text along the spine.

On the right you can see what the cover looks like, but with the Template layer turned on the book would be printed with most of the yellow showing and would probably have

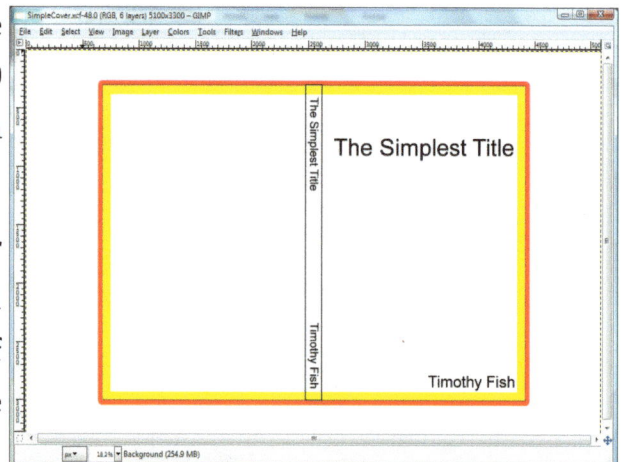

part of the red showing. Click the eye to turn off the Template layer and the image below is what you'll see:

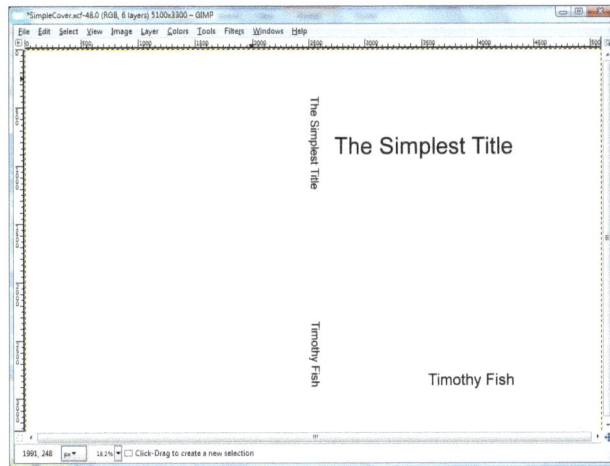

What you don't see yet are things like Back Cover Copy (BCC) and the ISBN barcode. Adding the BCC is just more of the same, but you may need to generate a barcode for the cover. Some companies will superimpose a barcode over your cover graphics, so you don't have to mess with it, other than you will need to know where they will be putting the barcode. If they provide a template, it should show where it falls.

There are several barcode generators out there. As far as free barcode generators go, I've had the most success with:

http://www.tux.org/~milgram/bookland

There is also a barcode generator built into Inkscape, but it doesn't include the price information and doesn't provide much in the way of help. When I've used the link above, it provided a zip file containing a PDF file. To import the PDF file into Gimp, just drag the file onto your image. An import window will pop up. Set the resolution to 300 dpi. You will need to use the copy tool to remove most of the white space and the barcode will be a little too large, but you can use the tools available in Gimp to position and resize the barcode to 2" wide by 1.2" high.

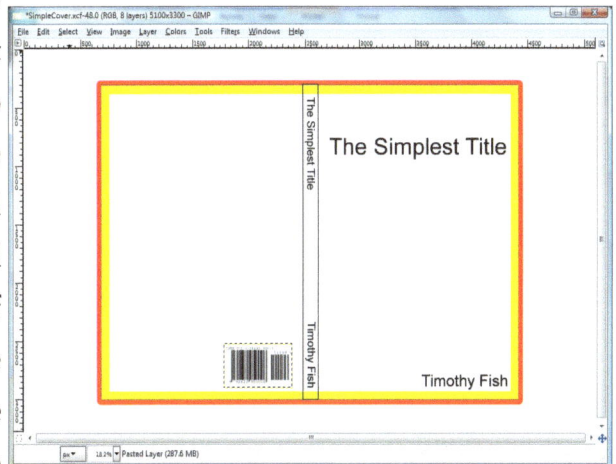

Ready For the Printer

In theory, you should be able to print the image you've created in Gimp to a PDF file using whatever PDF creation software you have available. If you don't have Acrobat Distiller, there are several free PDF creators available on the Internet and they all work pretty much the same way. But Gimp doesn't work well for printing. To get around this problem, when I'm ready to save the cover to PDF, I save the image as a .png file and I place the image in Microsoft Publisher, using a 17x11 page size. This has the added advantage of allowing me to use the same method whether I'm using Gimp or Inkscape and it also allows me to use publisher to add the text, if I like.

When printing to a PDF file, you must make sure that the size of the "paper" is the correct size. The image needs to come out as a single page in the PDF file. Other than that, it is as simple as printing anything else.

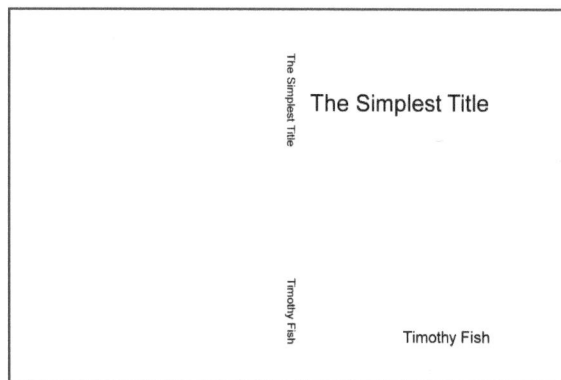

The Simplest Title

The Simplest Title

Timothy Fish

Timothy Fish

What's Really Important

It is very likely that most of the people who buy your book will not see the artwork in all of its glory until after they've made their purchase. These days, people will see a book cover online and that may be the basis by which they decide to take a closer look or ignore it all together. The images they see are almost always scaled down representations of the front cover. In many cases, the image is the size of a postage stamp. Take a look at our examples of bad covers again and see what you can tell about the book.

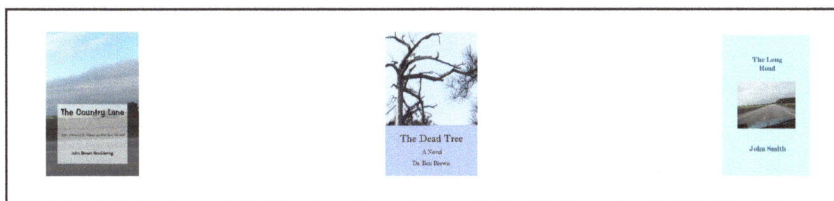

If your eyes are good, you may be able to make out the title. You can see the pictures, though you may not be sure what is in the picture. You can tell what color the images are. As you can tell, when the images are this small, we don't have much space to hook a reader.

We frequently see books on which the author's name is featured prominently on the front cover. If the author is famous, there is a good reason for that. The more famous authors have many fans who are eager to get their hands on the next book by that author. As they are browsing the Internet, if they happen to see the name of their favorite author on a postage stamp sized image and they don't recognize the book, they are going to click through to find out about this latest release. But since you are designing your own covers, it's doubtful you are a famous author. People like us want to whisper our names rather than shout them. In time, we may have reason for our name to take so much space, but not yet.

For unknowns like us, it will be either the title or the graphics that will have the greatest pull. That's just one more thing for our bad covers to suffer from. The graphics are generic and people can't see the title well enough to know what it is.

As we move forward, remember that even though there are many neat things we can do with a cover, if the cover obscures the title without giving us some other kind of hook, the cover will not help our book. Look for covers that highlight the title so people will remember the book.

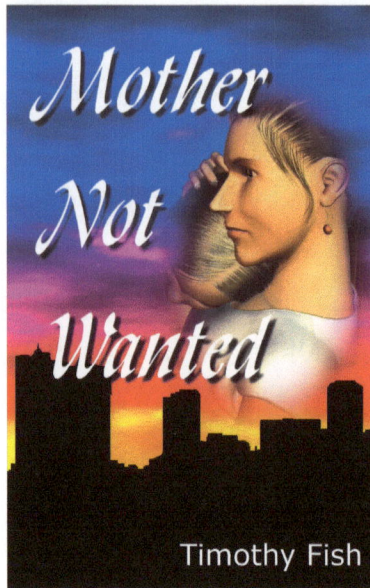

Timothy Fish

Clouds and a Sunrise

The cover you see above is one that I did for the book *Mother Not Wanted*. Everything you see is computer generated, including the people, but take a look at that sky. The sky over Fort Worth never looked like that. It's much easier to accomplish than you might think, so let's take a look at how to do it.

Using the same template we used before, let's start by selecting the Background layer and adding a White Layer, called Clouds. Then from the Filters menu select Render then Clouds and then Difference Clouds. (This will not work on a transparent layer.)

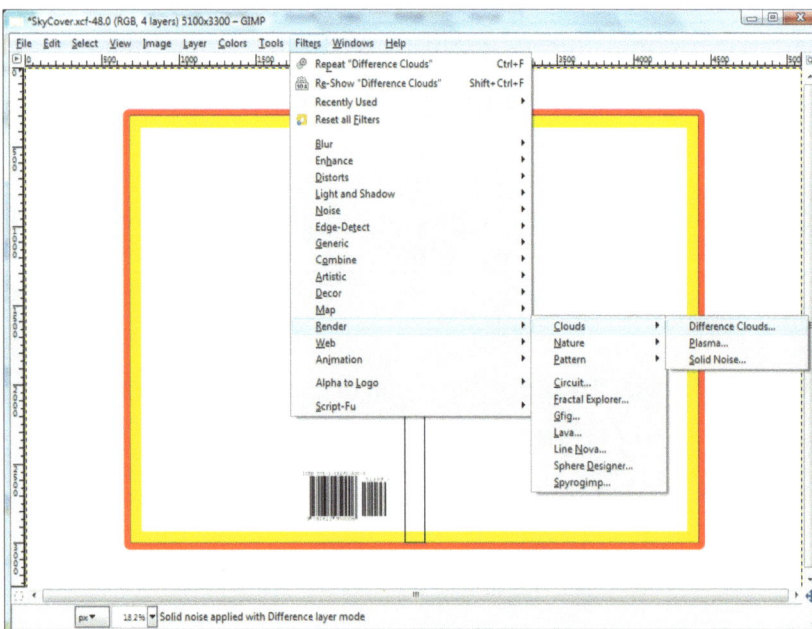

Use the settings shown here.

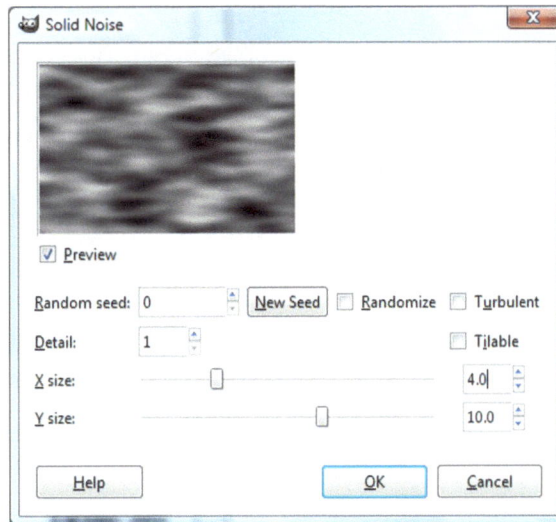

The result will be something that looks like the following:

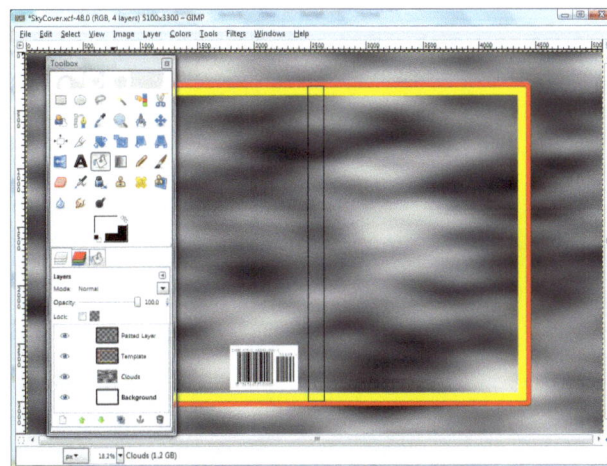

You can see that we're allowing the rendering to extend all the way to the edge of the page. We can ignore that portion because it will be trimmed during the printing process. If it is easier to let something extend all the way out then do that. If it is easier to stay nearer the boundaries then do that.

But we aren't quite where we wanted to be. At this point, the cover looks a little like clouds, but they are gray and ominous. The cover we started with has a background that looks more like a sunrise.

Select the Clouds lays and create a new layer. Call it SkyColor.

With the SkyColor layer selected, select the Blend tool and choose the gradient that is shown selected in the this image. You select the gradient by clinking on the gradient box on the Tool Options tab and finding the one you need. This Gradient is called Skyline.

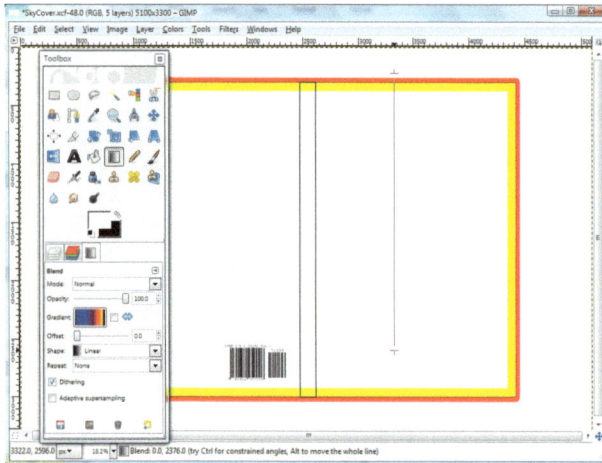

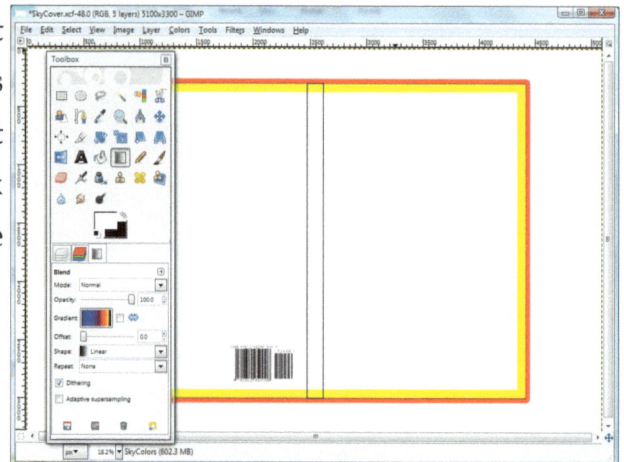

As is shown here, use the mouse to click with the gradient tool just above the top of the red line and drag a straight line down to about an inch from the bottom edge of the cover.

Once the gradient has been applied, the image will look like the one shown here. The colors look about right for what we're aiming for, but it still isn't quite right.

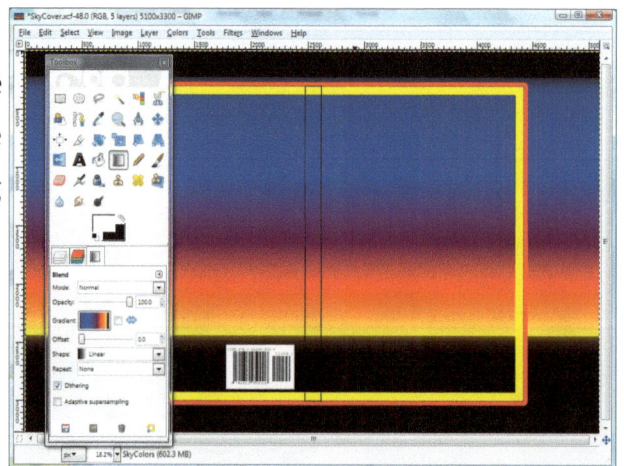

To get the look we want, we need only go to the Layers tab, and set the Mode of the SkyColor layer to Hard Light.

While you're messing with that setting, you might as well try some of the other modes too. Often, the best way to design a cover is to play with some the settings. You might try one thing and it looks terrible, but you try something else and it looks interesting.

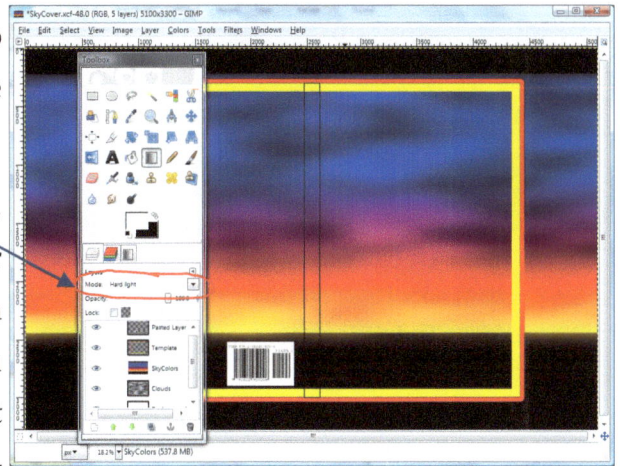

During the time that I was working on the cover we've mimicked here, I played with the colors quite a bit. I didn't find anything I liked better for *Mother Not Wanted*, but some of what I found gave me ideas that I might use for cover for other books.

While it may look like one of the simple things on the cover, the Fort Worth skyline took a significant amount of time to produce. Just to make things interesting, we'll use part of the Branson skyline to accomplish the same thing.

Some images work better than others. One of the problems we run into is that some of the things we want to be black are the same color as some of the things we want to be transparent. It is easy for a human to tell the difference, but we have to find a way to help the computer do the same.

First let's drag the image into our working cover so that Gimp will create a new layer with it in it. I've positioned the picture of Branson so the that hill in the background lines up with the beginning of the black in our background. And I've moved it far enough to the right that it lines up with the outer edge of the bleed line. All that is left to do is to select the sky, remove that area and paint the rest of it black.

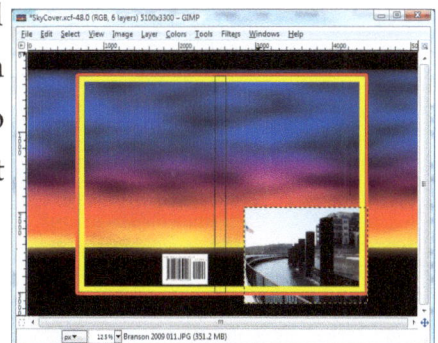

For this image, the Threshold tool will work nicely.

First, duplicate the layer the image is on.

Select the Threshold tool from Color|Threshold.

Use the sliders to adjust the black and white areas to where the areas you want to be black are black and those you went white are white. You won't get it exact, so just get it as close as possible. The rest will have to be colored by hand.

In the example, the white in the flag doesn't go completely black. We'll have to mess with that. The water also doesn't go black.

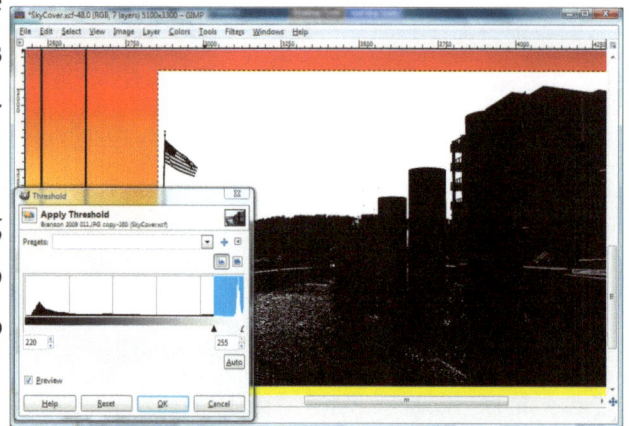

The easiest way to handle the big areas that didn't go black is to use the Free Select tool to encircle those area and then to use the Bucket Fill tool to fill the area with black. (Make sure the Bucket fill tool is set to fill the whole selection.)

After that, the only real problem area we have for this image is the flag.

Here's how it looks when we zoom in on it. The easiest solution appears to be to use the Paint Brush tool to cover the white that we don't want in the flag. It's best to avoid freehand when we can, but in this case it may be the best option.

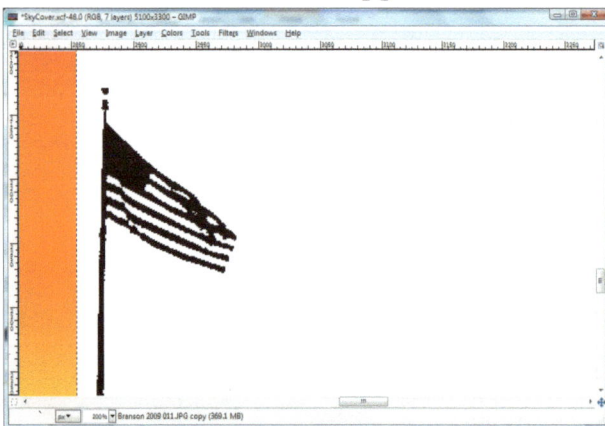

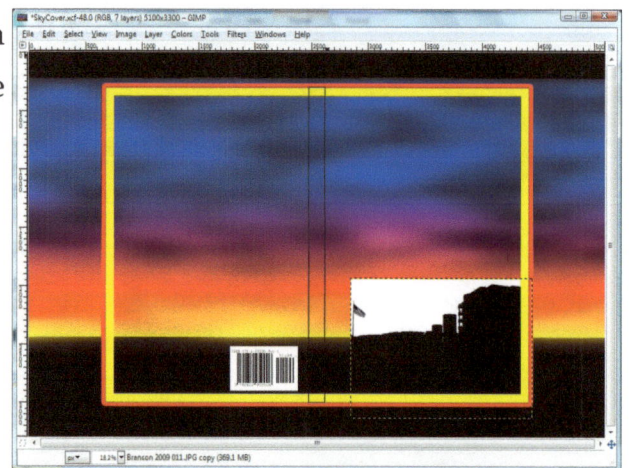

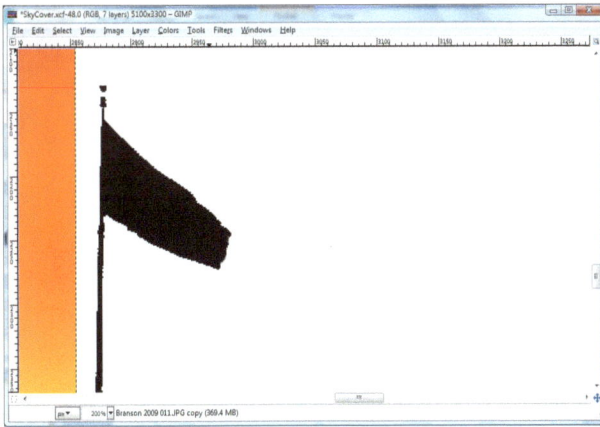

Here is the result of using the Paint Brush tool on the flag.

Once you are finished, zoom back out.

Right click on the layer in the Layer's tab and select Add Alpha Channel.

Use the Select by Color tool, and click on a white portion of the layer to select the non-black area.

Press the Delete key to remove the white and replace it with transparency.

To complete the black portion of the image, we want to darken that strip between the yellow and the black. With the Branson Layer selected, select Layer | Layer to Image Size.

Then use the rectangular selection tool to select the area at the bottom and fill the area with black using the Bucket Fill tool.

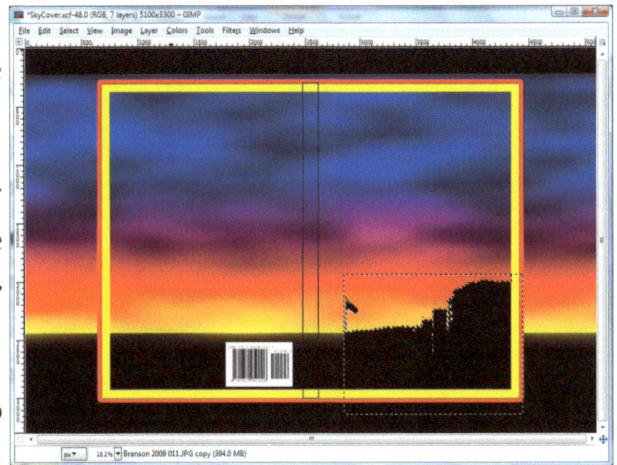

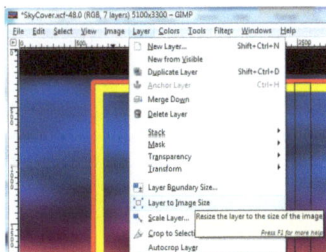

Short of having the text and the character's face on the cover, the cover is complete. But you'll notice that the symbolism in this cover is different. With the original cover, everyone who looks at it can tell that they are looking at the downtown area of a major city.

Some people may even recognize some of the buildings of the Fort Worth skyline, but the image here is of Branson and it doesn't immediately scream Branson when you see it. The most prominent feature is the flag. The symbolism is now telling us it is a school. Symbolism is something we must always keep in mind.

While we're here, let's use a different gra-

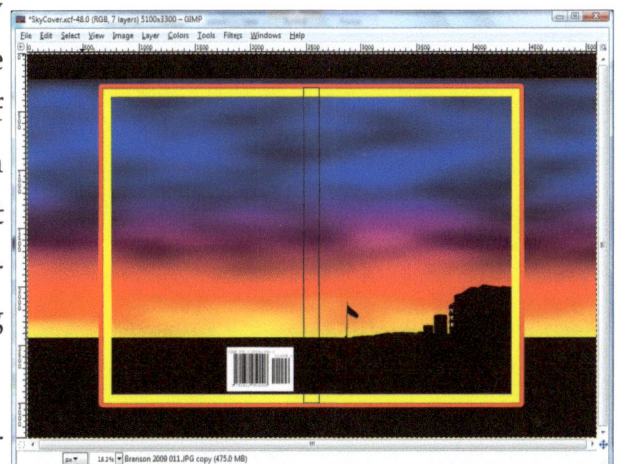

dient with the Blend tool. The gradient I used for the image to the right is the Deep Sea gradient. Notice how different the cover looks with just a change in the colors. What we did before gave us an indication that there was fire on the horizon, but this cover is cold and foreboding. All we need is a title, an author, and a few characters and we just might have a mystery on our hands.

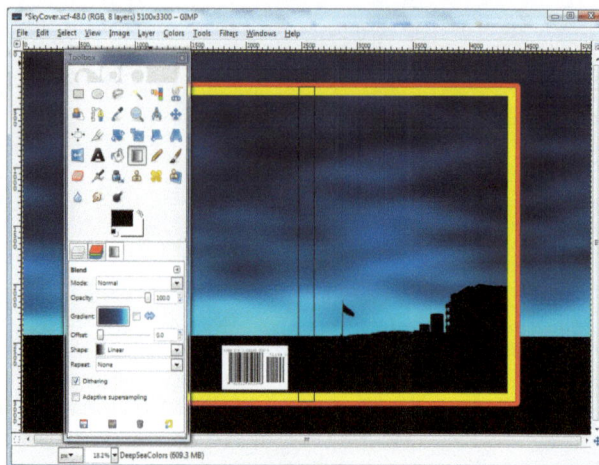

Faces

There's something about the human face that forces us to take notice. In fact, our brains process faces differently than they process other visual stimuli. Perhaps that's why so many books have nothing but a human face on the cover. One example of a cover like that is the one below:

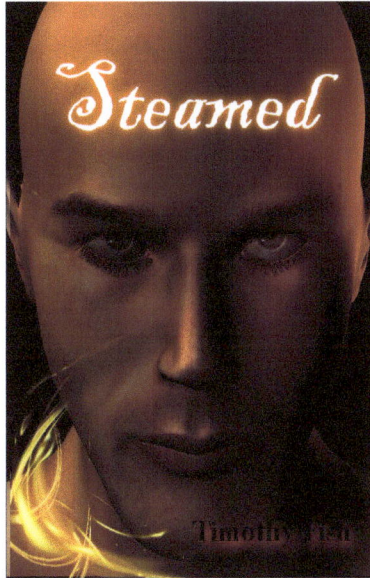

Anytime we use a face on a cover, the eyes play an important role. In this example, the eyes are looking straight at the camera. This guy is clearly not one of those people who believes you shouldn't look into the camera lens. Even though his head is slightly down in relation to the camera, his eyes look straight out at us and it makes us uneasy.

A cover like this is intended to make us feel a little uneasy. It implies that it is that kind of a story. Everything about the cover is dark. The man's face is in shadow. The background is black. There's the hint of fire off in the corner and behind the text. If the cover fits the story, it takes place in a dark part of our world. Perhaps it takes place at night. Perhaps it takes place in some darkened alleys. If your book has that kind of story, then this is the kind of cover you need.

So, as we did before, let's look at what it would take to reproduce this cover. We begin with a model. Models come from a number of different places. If you know how to bribe them you can talk your friends into being models. There is 3D software out there that will produce decent results, which is what I

did here. But many of the covers you will see have images that were sold as stock photos. There are several websites out there that do nothing but sell stock photos. Based on some of the prices I've seen, you could probably purchase a photo that's similar to this one for around $75. And it may run you as much as $150. But that beats the conversation you might have at Christmas time if the character with your cousin's face kills his mother in your book. If you can afford it, always go with the largest sized file available. In a case like this, where we need the image to fill the whole page, using an 1800x2700 pixel image would be too small for a 6x9 inch book. We'll need the larger size because we need enough to spill over into the bleed area. Otherwise, we risk seeing the edge of the image on our cover.

As you can see, the first thing I did was to drop the picture of my guy onto the template. You might want to do some editing first, so that the image is the proper size. Unlike the stuff we did before, this time the image extends not only through the red line into the area that will be trimmed, but it extends into the live area of the spine and the back cover. We will have to deal with that. For now, we will ignore it. Our main concern is the front cover.

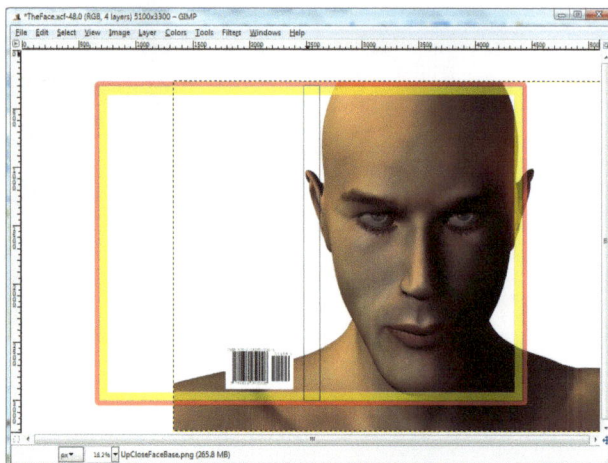

One of the first things we notice about our actor is that he is a little too white. He almost looks like he's standing in front of a mirror in a bathroom. He certainly doesn't have the coloring we saw on the cover example. To fix that, we can use the Blend tool.

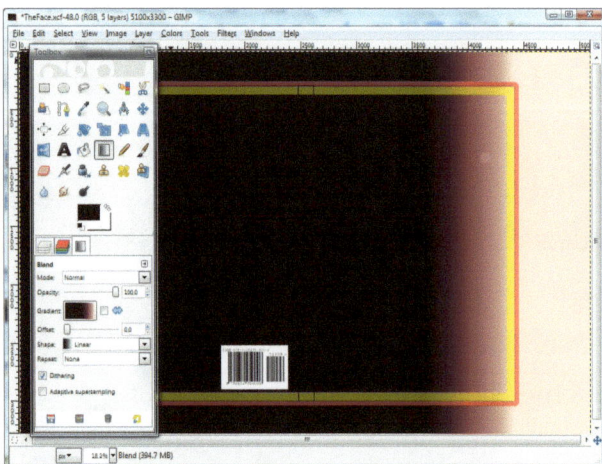

Create a new transparent layer above the layer for our guy.

Using the Dark 1 gradient, click and drag the Blend tool from his ear closest to the spine to the other ear. The result should look something like what you see here.

Change the mode of that layer to Overlay.

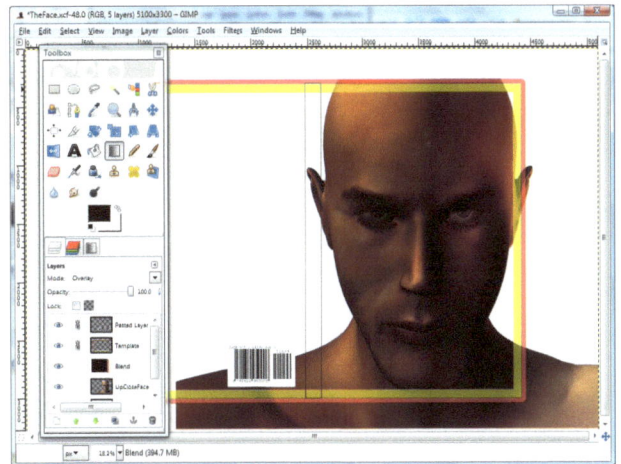

It looks a little more like the original, but it's a little hard to tell.

Select the Background layer and use the Bucket Fill tool to fill the layer with black.

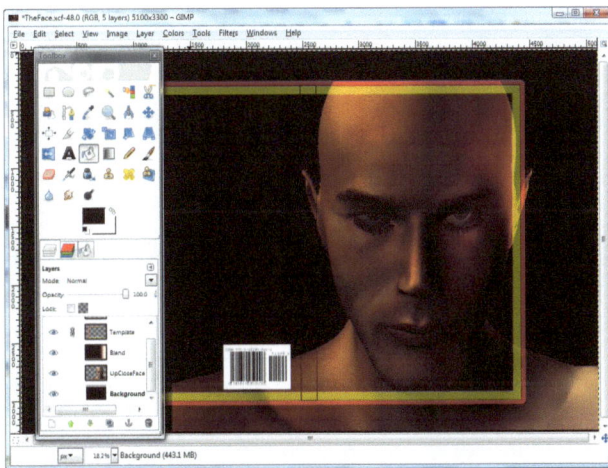

The next thing on our list to do is to create something that resembles fire. Fire is difficult if we try to shape it too much. Fire is random, and yet predictable. It is a blend of color. We don't want to draw the flames by hand, so we'll settle for something that gives the impression of fire.

To begin, create a New image that is 120x120 pixels.

Fill the background with black, then create a new Trans-

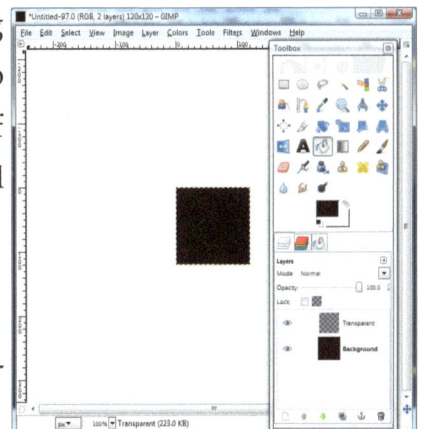

parent layer.

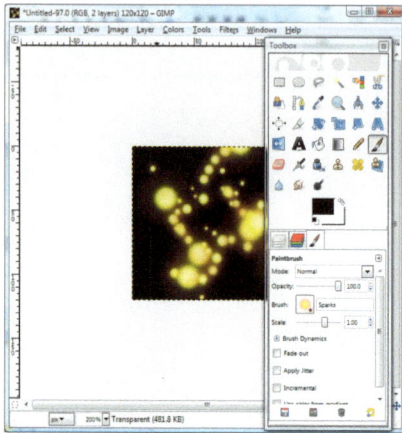

Select the Paint Brush tool.

Select the Sparks Brush.

Use the brush to paint some randomly sized sparks on your drawing area.

Select Filters|Distorts|iWarp.

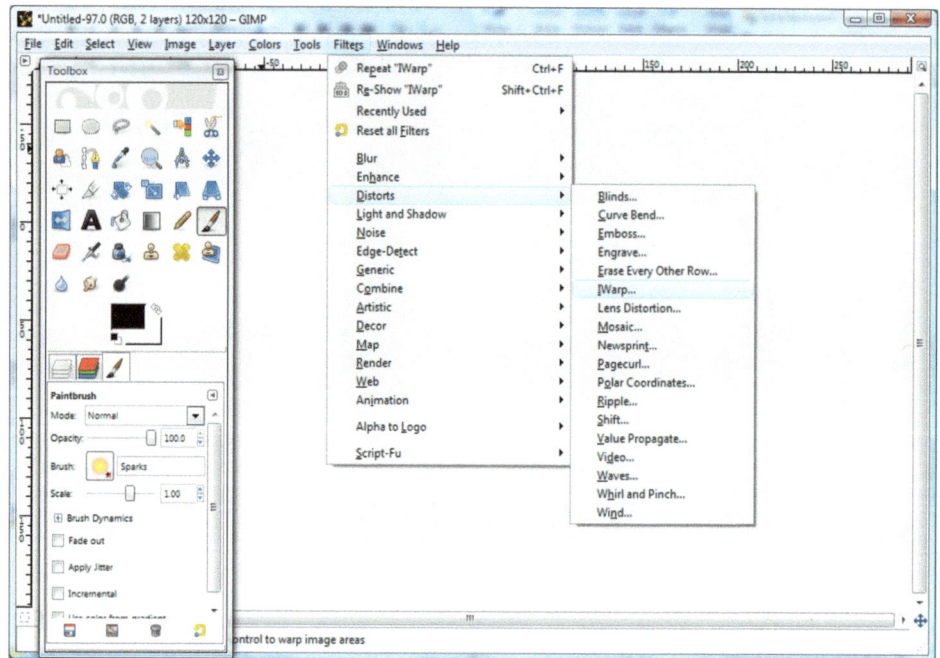

Use the various deform tools to Swirl and move the sparks until they begin to look a little like fire.

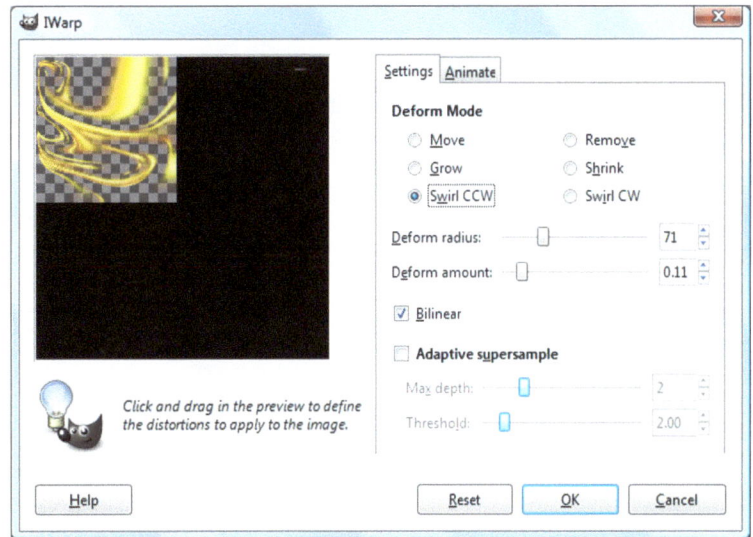

My attempt looks like the following:

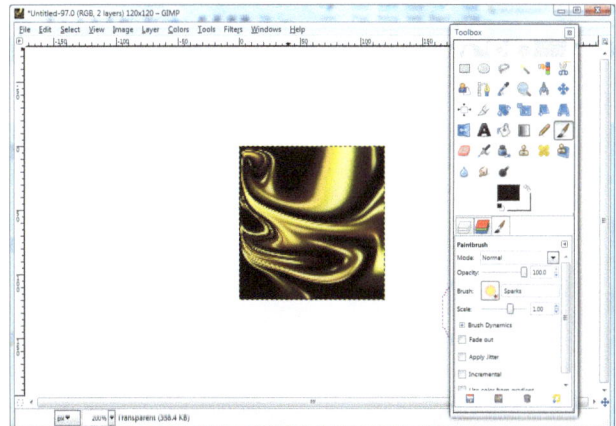

Delete the Background and scale the image to 1200x1200

Copy the image and paste it as a new layer into our cover.

Next, reposition the "flames" where you want them.

Then select the eraser tool and change the brush to one of the fuzzy brushes.

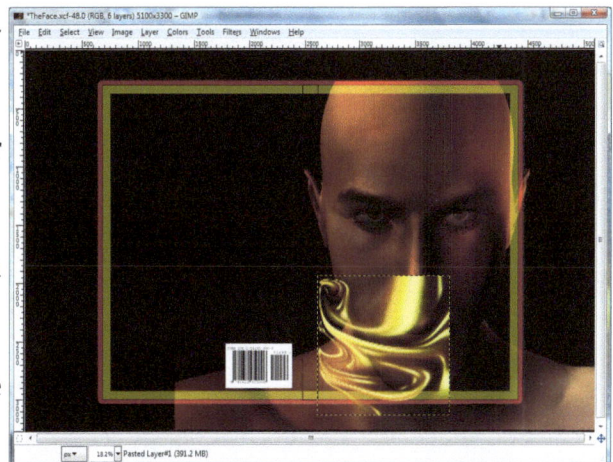

Using it as a fuzzy brush eraser, remove everything from the pasted layer that doesn't look like a flame.

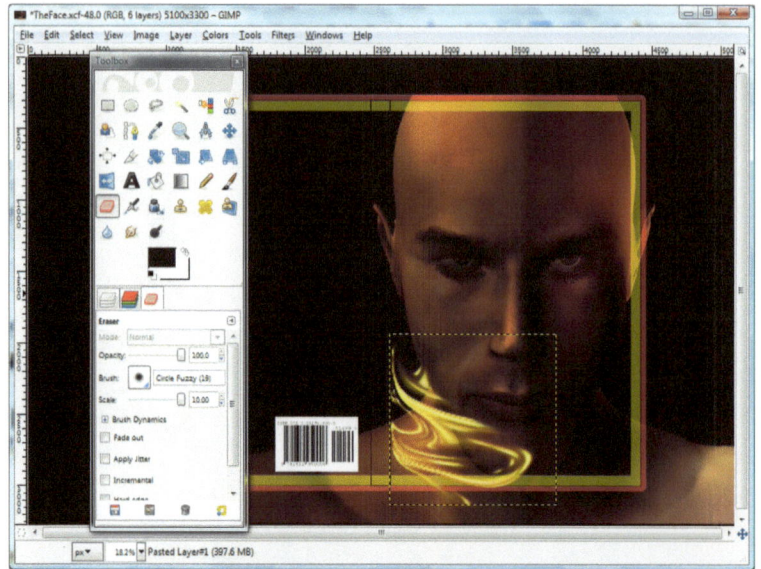

It's starting to look like we have flames, but when we view the flames at 100%, we have a problem. Because we scaled up from a smaller image, we have a jaggedness to the flame. We don't want this on the book.

Since we're working with something that doesn't have sharp lines, there is a fairly simple solution. We can blur the flames to the point that the jagged edges are smooth.

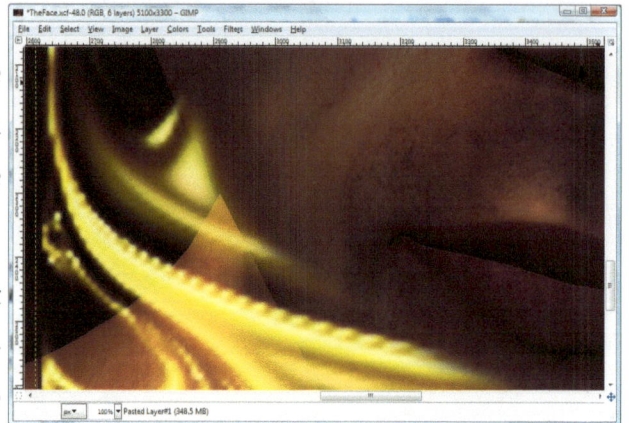

Select Filters|Blur|Gaussian Blur

With no blur applied, the preview looks like this.

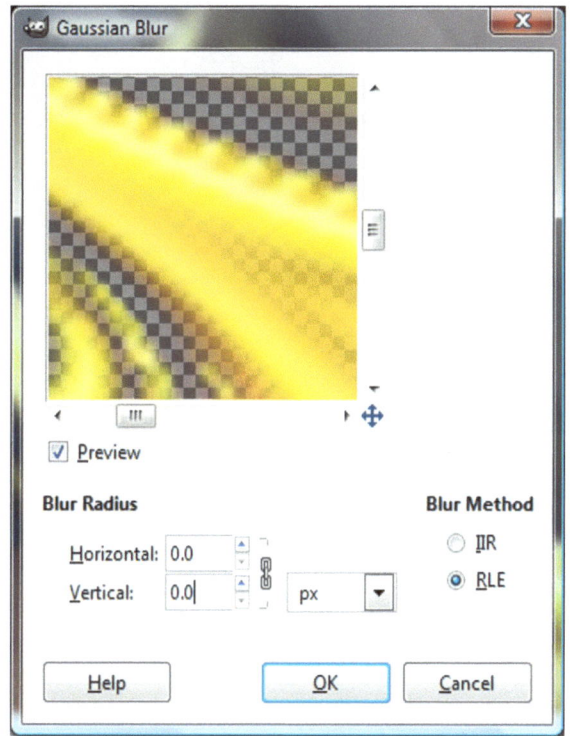

With Blur Radius of 25 both Horizontal and Vertical, the preview looks like this. Increase the radius until the jaggedness goes away.

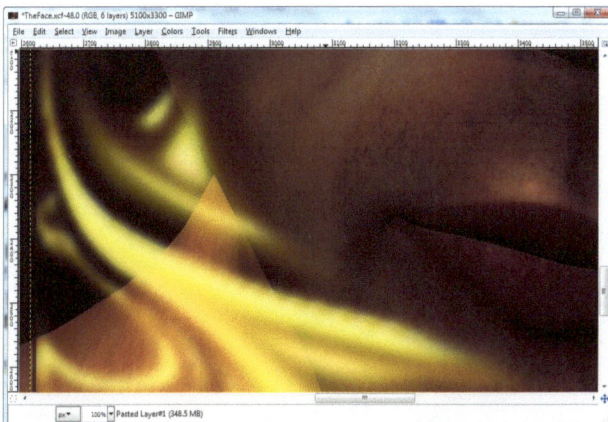

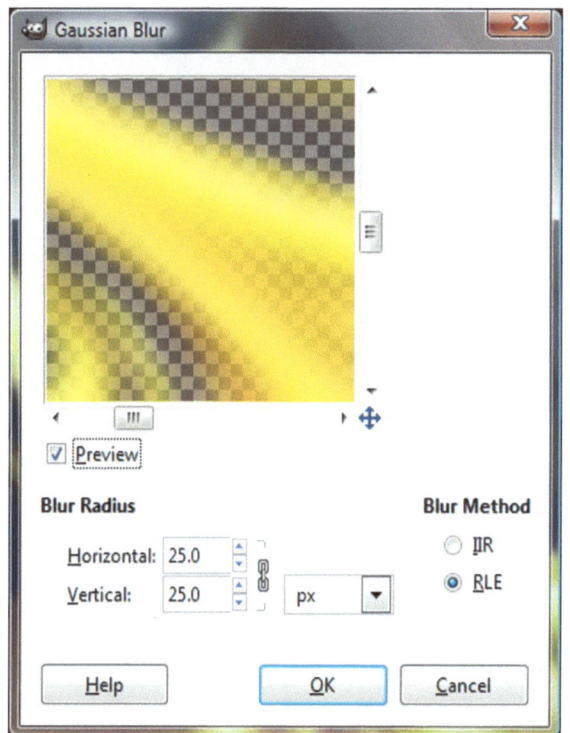

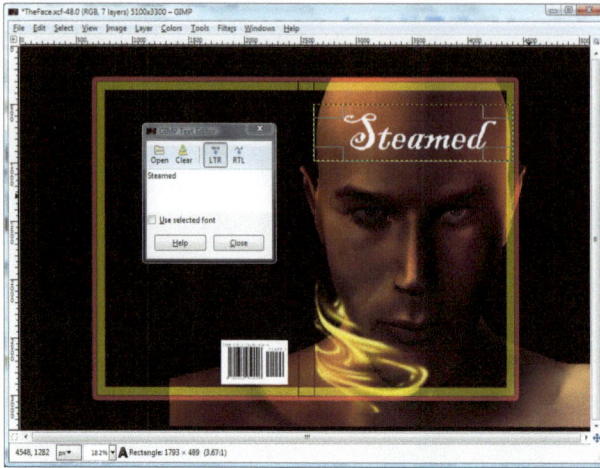

The title lettering seems at first to be just simple white text, but as soon as we apply the white text to the image we find that it seems to be a little bit more flat than we were expecting.

The text in the original has a drop shadow applied to it. In Gimp, as with most of the rendering tools, we find the Drop Shadow tool on the Filters menu.

With the text layer active, go to Filters|Light and Shadow|Drop Shadow.

Normally, with a Drop Shadow, we would set the X and Y Offsets to positive numbers and the Color to black or dark gray so that it appears that a light is shining on the text from above and to the left of the text. Here, what we need to do is to set the Offsets to 0 and the color to yellow. We also set the Blur radius to 50, so that the "shadow" will spill out from underneath the letters.

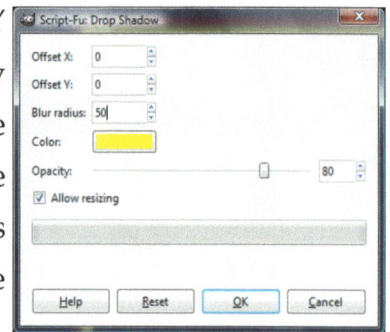

Here is the result:

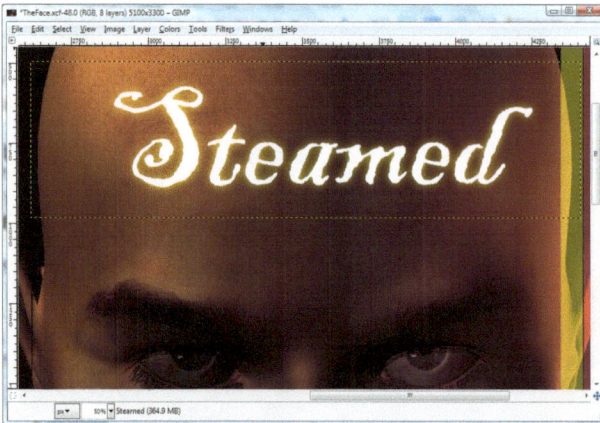

To give it a little more definition, we can apply another Drop Shadow to the letters. This time use red and a Blur Radius of 25. With the size of image we're working with, this will give the letters a hint of a red border.

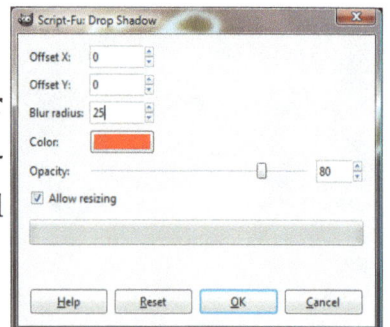

32

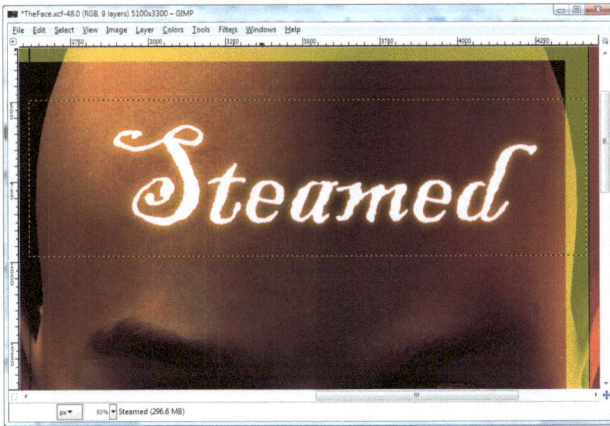

We can use a similar technique with the author's name. To reduce the prominence and to make it somewhat interesting, I chose to use black for the lettering. Where the name is placed, the text has very low contrast with the image. Applying a drop shadow will help to increase the contrast and make the letters more apparent. This is a trick you can use anywhere you have letters that are at low

contrast with the image. White letters with a white background, for example, become readable when a drop shadow is applied.

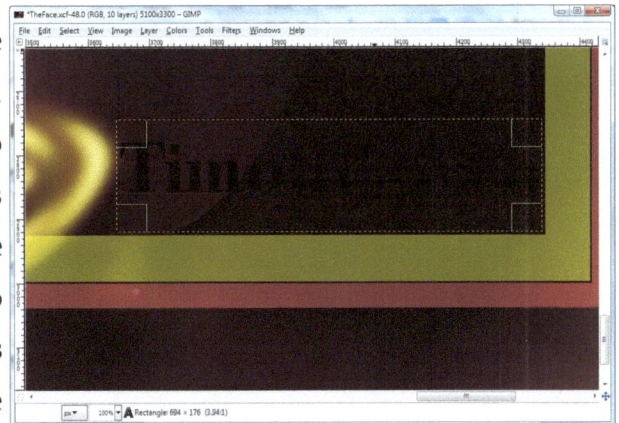

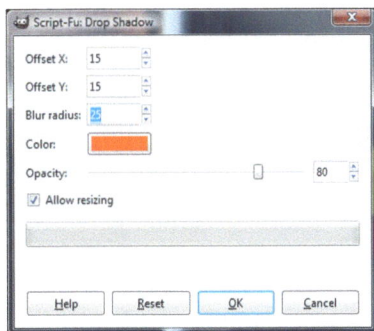

An offset of 15 in both directions and an orange color will give us this result for the author's name.

The contrast still isn't so high that the name stands out, but it is readable enough

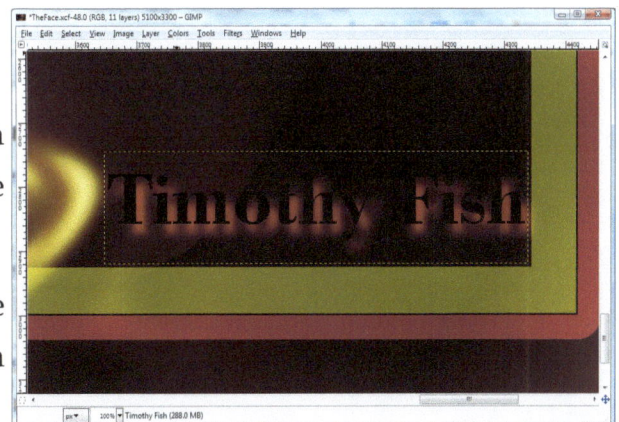

that people who want to know who wrote the book can tell.

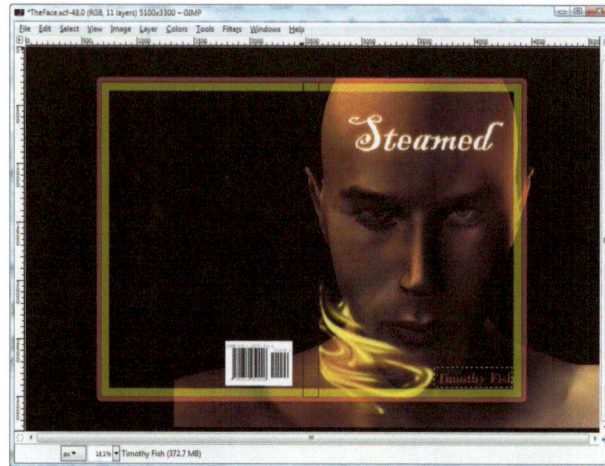

At this point, it is good to take a step back and assess what is left to do. We still have the back to mess with. But I can also tell that our flames are still somewhat jagged. Before moving on to the back and spine, we should take care of that. I need only to select that layer and apply more blur to the flames. The nice thing about flames is that blurriness doesn't hurt them much.

Now, moving to the back and spine we see that our guy's shoulder ends abruptly. To the right is what our cover looks like trimmed. Looking at it like this, the shoulder looks like it just needs to be rounded, but something we've got to remember is that unless someone lays our book out flat, they are never going to see the cover in this way. The image below is how the back looks

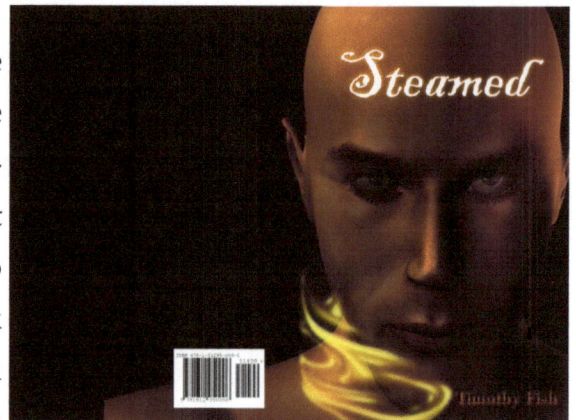

by itself.

Without the context of the face on the front cover, having a guy's shoulder just sticking out there like that is rather weird looking. It is further complicated by the barcode being there.

Because of the nature of the image on the front, our best solution for this problem is to cover the offending shoulder with black. To do that, create a Transparent Layer that is positioned above everything except the barcode.

With the Rectangular Select tool, select an area that includes all of the back cover and spine, but doesn't include the front cover.

Use the Bucket Fill tool to fill the area with black.

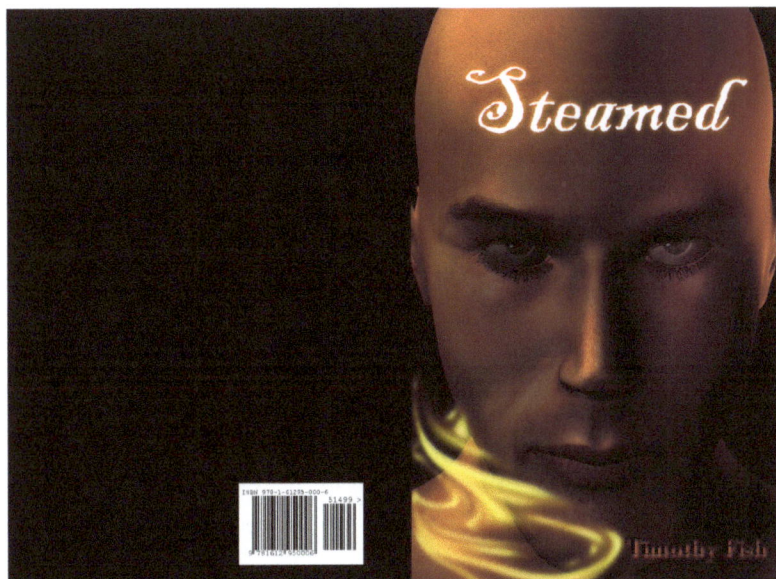

This gives use the result shown here. To get a better idea of what the front will look like, look at the following:

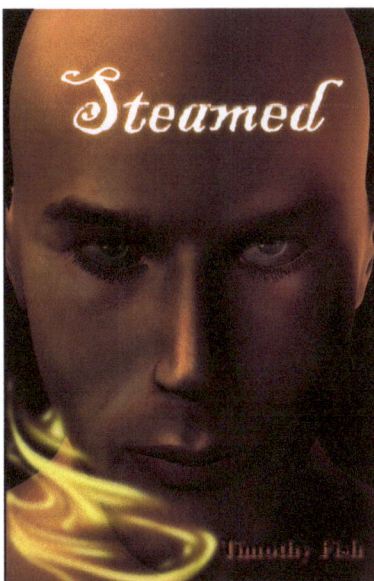

The Rule of Thirds

You may have noticed that while we were working on that last cover, it was a little easier on the eyes when we were working on the full cover than when we were working with the front cover alone. The reason for this has to do with the graphic composition rule known as the Rule of Thirds. The basis for the rule is the theory that a graphic composition will look better if the key elements are placed at the intersection of lines drawn at 1/3 and 2/3 of the width and height.

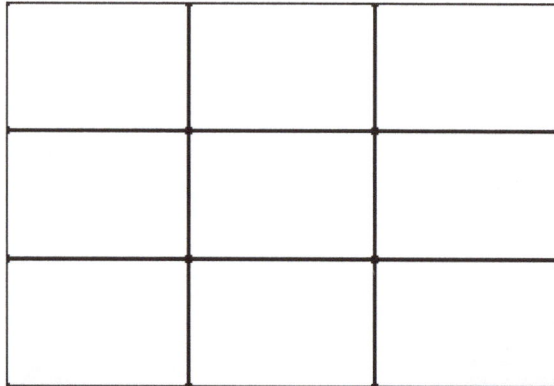

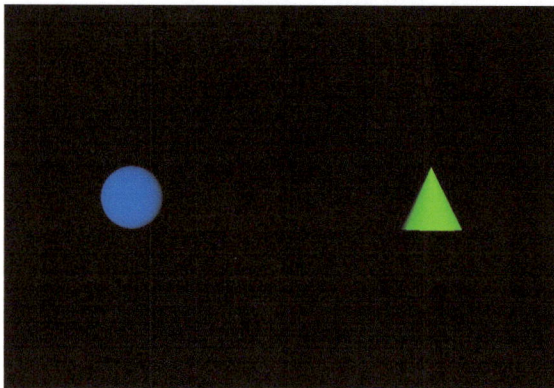

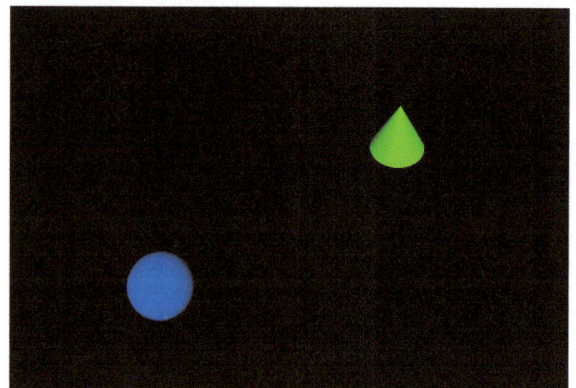

If the theory is true, then most people will find the images on the right more interesting than the images on the left because the objects appear on the intersections, rather than centered as they are in the image on the left.

Perhaps you aren't convinced by simple shapes. Compare these two figures, one centered and the other placed at the intersections. The second is naturally more interesting. And just in case you're wondering where this guy is in relation to the thirds, look at the following:

Now, let's look at how this applies to book cover design in particular. In the image below, notice how close the eyes are to the upper two intersections. In fact, if we hadn't left so much space on the guy's forehead for the title, they would line up exactly. The corners of his mouth also line up. The human face is a perfect example of a composition that uses the rule of thirds. So, it shouldn't seem odd to us that it works. God created the rule when he created everything else.

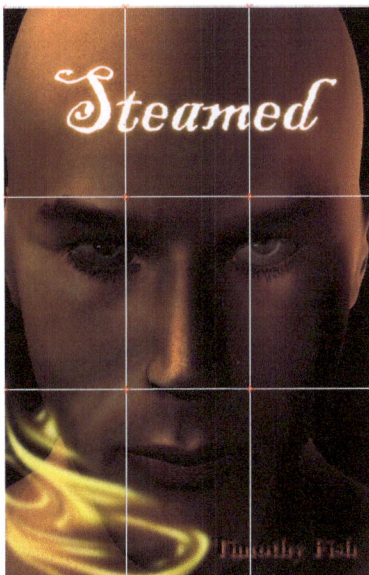

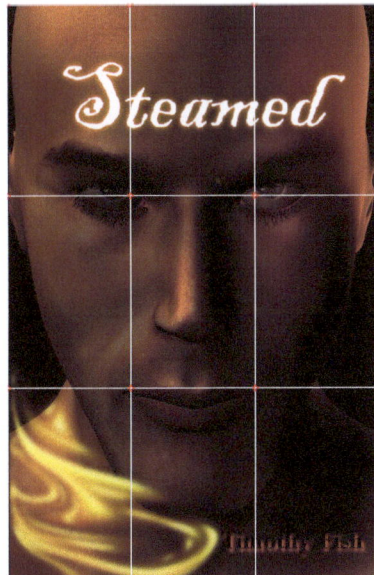

But there is a limited number of covers we can design that have a close-up of the human face. We frequently see covers with a couple of people on the front. Particularly with romances, we'll see the point of view female character in the foreground and the male character some distance behind her. If we applied the Rule of Thirds very strictly to a cover like that, we would likely have character placement similar to what you see to the left. But that isn't what we see. Instead, we're more likely to see placement like what we see in the image on the right. The woman's face may fall on one of the intersections, but the man's face does not. It is close, but it isn't there.

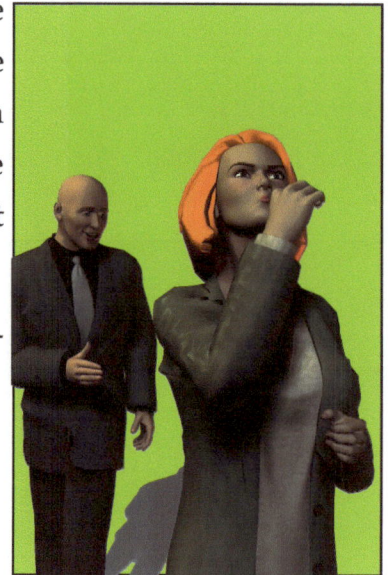

In images, the woman's face is almost always the money face.

The Romance Novel

There are many romance novels that follow the theme of one or two people with a background that is supposed to portray the area in which the story takes place. In Amish fiction, for example, you're likely to see the picture of a model wearing Amish clothing and a white bonnet. You may see a young Amish man in the background wearing a straw hat. Behind them, you may see a wagon or a simple house or a barn. In historical fiction, you may see a woman wearing an elaborate dress with a palace in the background. In contemporary fiction, you may just see a woman sitting with the water and a boat dock behind her. When you see them as a pattern, you can see that they look very much like the image below:

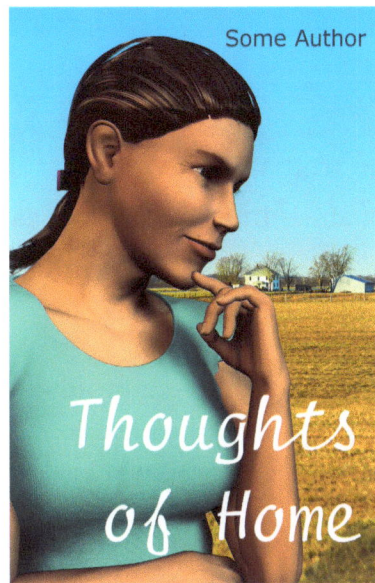

If you've understood how to do the things we've done with the other covers, it is well within your grasp to paste a high resolution stock photo in the background of an image and then paste the image of a woman in the foreground. The reason I want us to look at the creation of this cover is because it will allow me to demonstrate some techniques that you may find useful.

Take a look at the original image for the background. Aside from the slight change in coloring, what you should notice here is that the original image isn't large enough to use for the cover. There isn't enough sky and there isn't enough dirt. We also have the problem that the farmhouse is too close to the center. Even if the image were wide enough as it is, as soon as we push it over where we want it, there

will be an edge in the middle of our cover.

Now look at the image of the woman that was used in the foreground. The image on the cover has a different color of shirt. In this case, that is a very easy change to make. In fact, we can easily mess with the color of her shirt until we're satisfied that is goes with the background the best that it can.

As with the other covers, we begin with the template we created earlier. The first thing we need to add to that is the image of the farmhouse. Even though the farmhouse will be near the vertical center, I lined up the center window with the Rule of Thirds line. We will end up with the woman on the one on the left and the farmhouse on the one on the right.

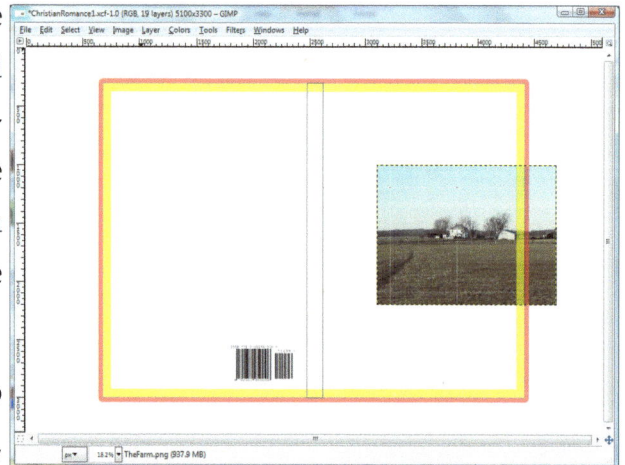

Now, we know that the woman is going to cover up the edge on the left of the picture, but with an image like this, in which the shadows aren't clearly defined, and there is a lot of stuff that can be repeated, it is fairly easy to extend the picture to the left. We want the hills in the background to look like they belong, we want the colors to match and we need more dirt.

To accomplished this, first, make a duplicate layer of the farmhouse.

Use the Flip tool to flip the duplicate layer from left to right.

Move the layer to the left until the edge of the original lines up with that of the duplicate.

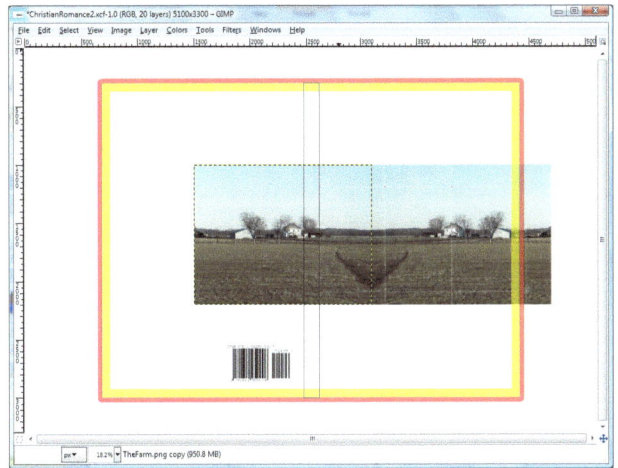

Because we want to work on it as one image, right click the upper farmhouse layer and select Merge Down to combine the layers.

The biggest indication of us splicing the image like that is the big V in the middle of the field. Even though the woman will be covering it up, let's correct that. The Clone tool is ideal for that.

Select the tool.

Hold the Ctrl key down while clicking in a part of the field that doesn't have this dark streak in it. Try to get a spot that is at the same vertical position as where you'll start painting.

Release the Ctrl key.

Paint over the area of the streak you want to hide.

You may need to increase the scale of the brush with the scale slider so that it is large enough for the high resolution images we are working with.

You can remove all of it, if you would like.

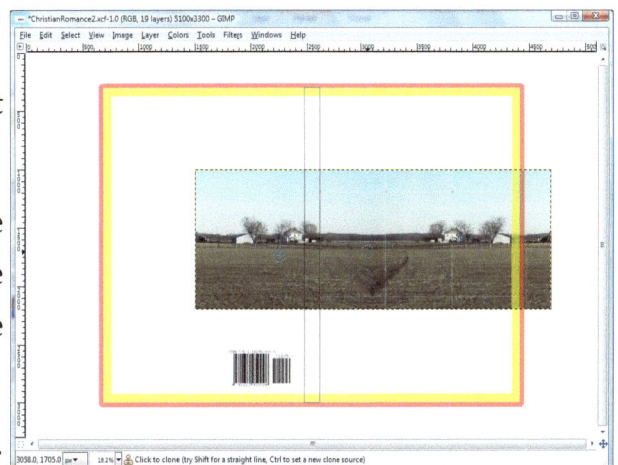

I chose to leave one side of the V because that line was in the original image. I just didn't want it looking like a V.

We can use a similar technique to finish out the rest of the field.

First, increase the size of the Layer to the image size, by selecting Layers | Layer to Image Size.

The Clone tool worked well where we could copy a part of the ground without resizing, but we run into a problem. It won't work well in a case where we need the ground to extend closer to the camera. The ground close to the camera should appear to have larger dirt clods than the ground closer to the fence. The Perspective Clone tool will allow us to clone the ground like before, but it will resize the dirt by the appropriate amount as we near the camera.

When we select the tool, we first must use the Modify Perspective mode to define the perspective of the image. Gimp has no way of knowing what the perspective of an image is until we tell it. In the Modify Perspective mode, click and drag in the image. You should see a box with angled lines. Adjust the handles until the box looks like it is lying flat on the ground.

In comparison to the picture, the box should look like it is a rectangle on the ground. With some images, you can take clues from objects you know are rectangular and aligned to the camera. If you have a road or sidewalk, for example, you could align your perspective with it and extend the road into the distance. Here, we just have to eyeball it.

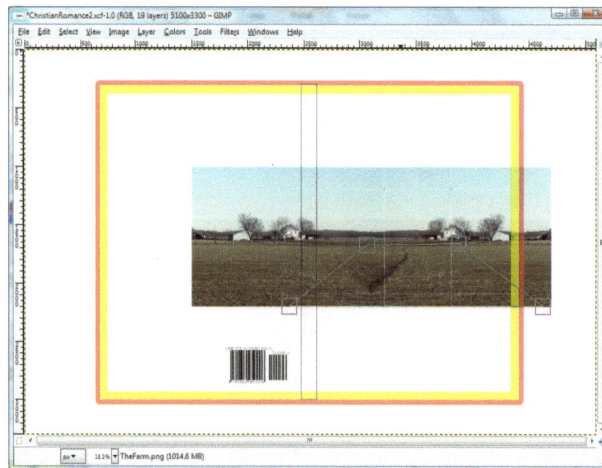

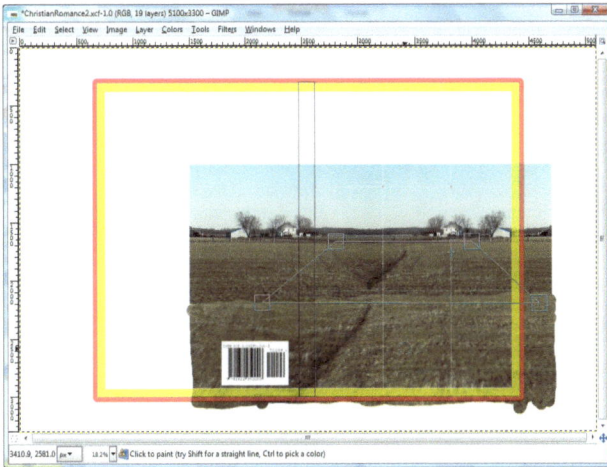

After switching to the Perspective Clone mode, we do like we did with the Clone tool.

Press Ctrl and click on the area you want to clone.

With the scale pushed up to the max, paint in the area of the cover that needs dirt.

Be sure to extend past the red line.

As you can see, there is a slight difference in coloring where we began the clone and the original. For something like this, a quick way to adjust that is to Ctrl click again, but this time a mouse's height above the line. Set the opacity of the Perspective Clone tool to about 40 and run the mouse along that line until they blend.

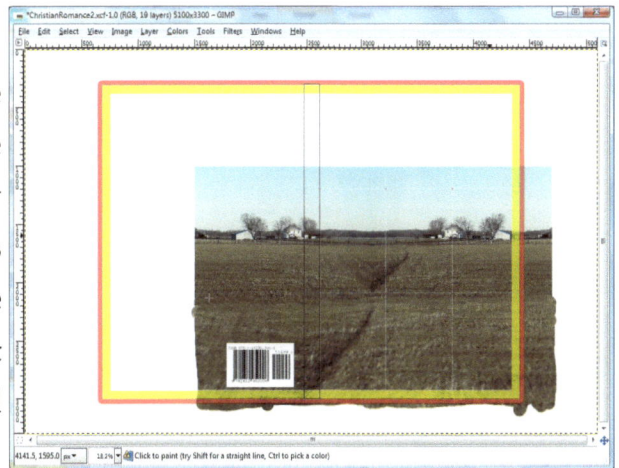

For the sky, we don't have anything that we can copy. The best way to fix the sky is to select everything we want to be sky and repaint it to our satisfaction.

Select the sky using the Select By Color tool . It won't select everything at once, so Shift click to add areas to the selection. Once you've completed that, you will have some areas that shouldn't be included that are in the selection. Use the other selection tools to remove areas by Ctrl clicking. Please note that you must release the Ctrl key once you have clicked and before you drag or the tool will function differently than you might expect.

Shift click with the Rectangular Selection tool and drag out a box to include the area above the image that we want to be part of the sky as well.

Once you are happy with your selection, select Select|Save to Channel from the menus. This will allow you to go back to that selection at a later time, by choosing it from the Channels tab and converting it to a selection.

Select the Layer with the image on it again.

Use the Color Picker tool to pick a color near the top of the hills. Ctrl click with the tool to pick a color near the top edge of the image.

Click on the Background color selector in the Toolbox and increase the Saturation of the color you picked near the top edge.

With the Blend tool click and drag from near just below the top of the hills to just above the top of the red line.

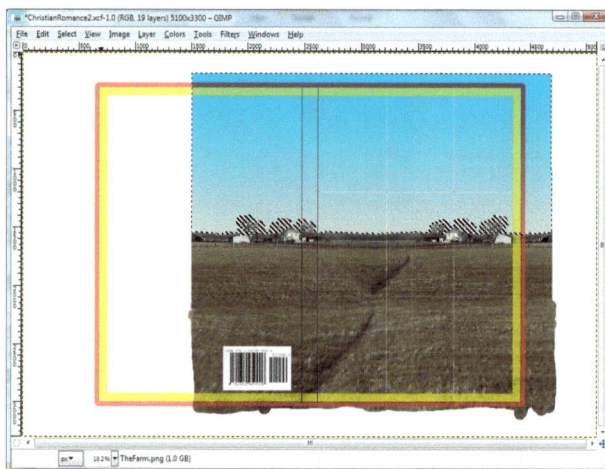

One of the things we can do to help the image is to adjust the Saturation. We can do that by selecting Colors|Hue-Saturation from the menus.

Here I pushed the Saturation slider all the way to the right. This gives he image a bit of a fanciful look. You can also use this tool to adjust the hue and the lightness of the image.

If you think the image is too bright or too

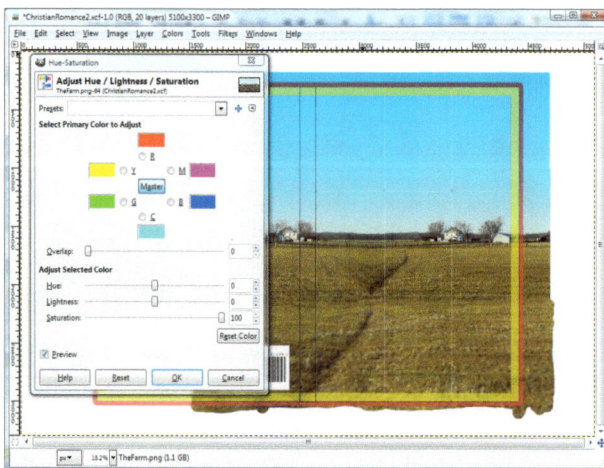

dark, this is the place to work on it.

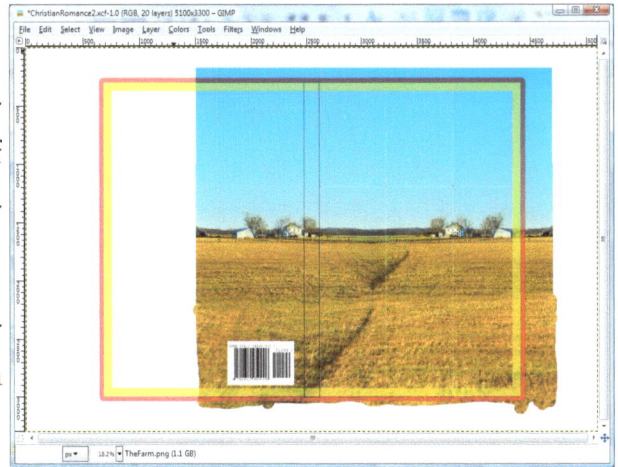

The image to the right is the result of maximizing the Saturation slider twice. Instead of brown and boring, the image is now beginning to look bright and sunny.

With the coloring of the background adjusted, we can now go to work on the woman on our cover.

Here's what she looks like when we first paste her in.

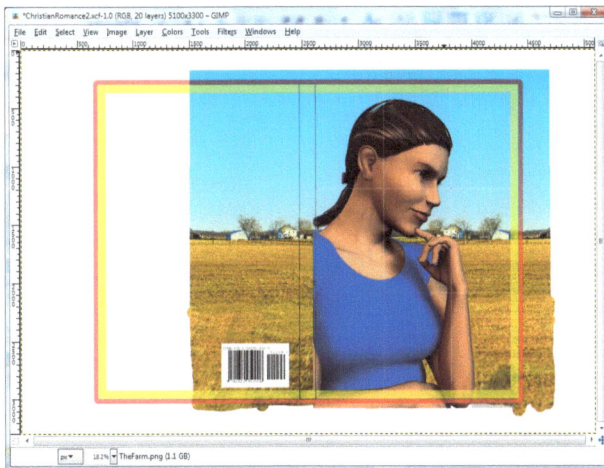

Yellow and blue are complimentary colors, so this doesn't look bad, but suppose we want to try her with different colored shirts. This woman is computer generated, so we could go back and regenerate her with different colors. If she were a living model, we could have the model change clothes several times during the photo shoot, which would cost money, but what if it were a stock photo? You might have found the perfect picture with the perfect pose, but the woman's shirt is the wrong color. Using the same tool we used to change the saturation of the farm, we can change the color of the woman's shirt.

Select Colors|Hue-Saturation again with the woman's layer active.

The woman's shirt is blue, so if we select the radio for the blue color, the Hue, Lightness and Saturation settings will be applied to her shirt. One of the nice things about this particular picture is that nothing else is blue, so we don't have to use the selection tools to limit the use of this tool. Blue and Green work well that way because flesh doesn't have those colors in them.

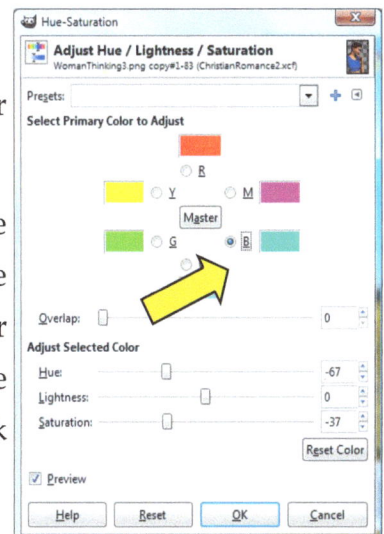

You've probably seen how that your favorite weatherman stands in front of a green or blue screen when he is pointing to the weather systems on the various maps. This works in a similar way.

Using a Hue of –67, a Lightness of 0, and a Saturation of –37, gives us the color of shirt used in the original image.

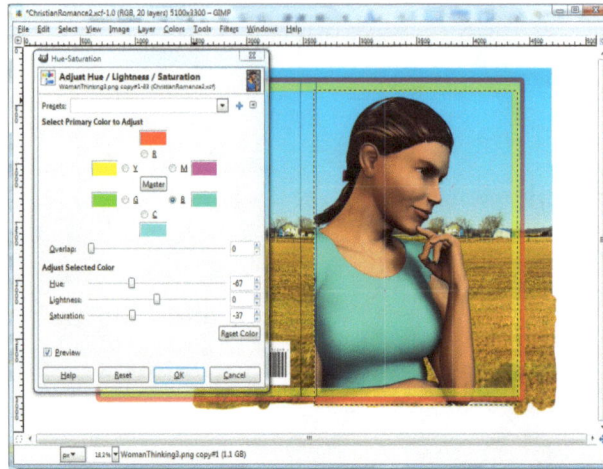

Or maybe we think it should be red.

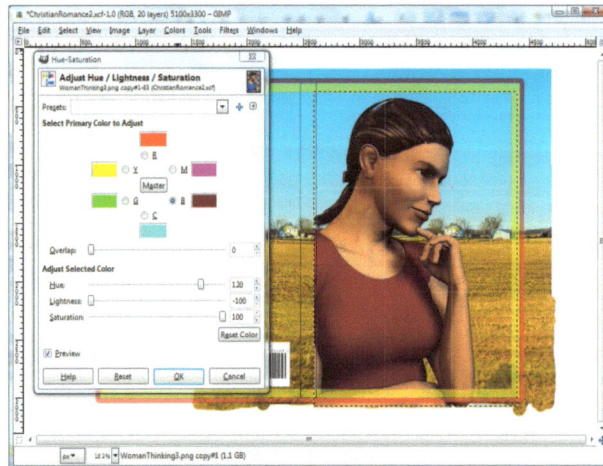

We can adjust the colors until we're happy with what we see.

With a little cleanup and some text, the cover is complete.

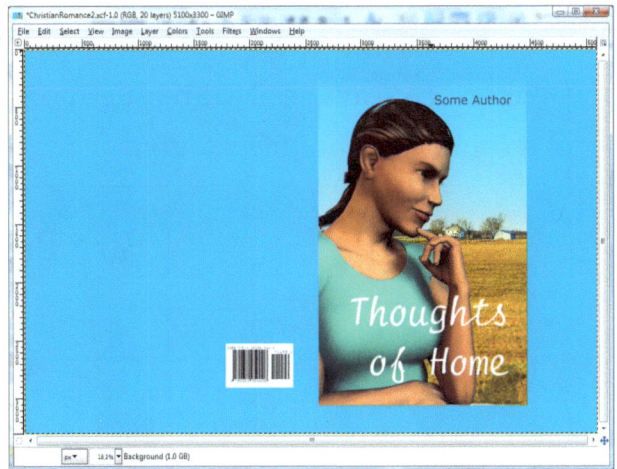

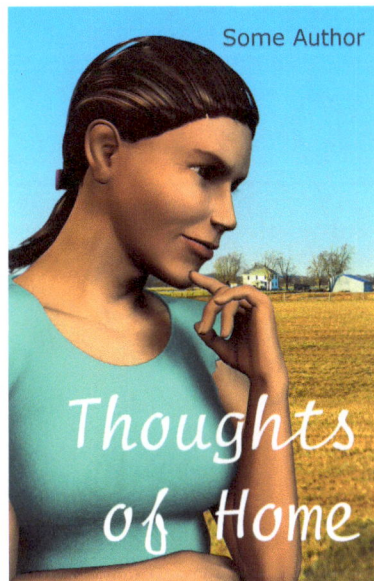

Cover Design With Inkscape

We don't always need the most elaborate covers. There are times when a simple image and the title are all we need to convey the message.

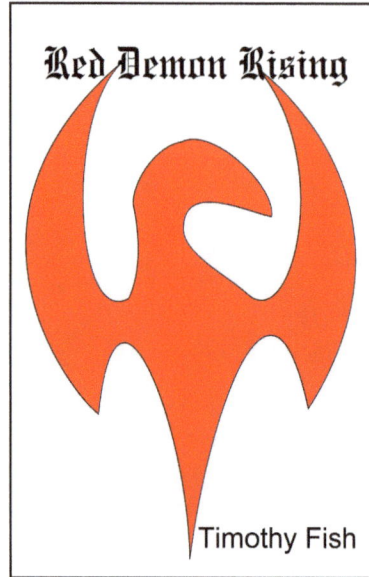

What I like about this cover is that it is so simple that it stands out. But it's not simple like child's art. The lines are too smooth for that. No, this is simple in a way that tells us that the cover designer intended the cover to look like that.

You could use Gimp to design a cover like that, but a vector graphics program like Inkscape is a better choice for a cover like this. Gimp has some limited vector graphics capability, but it was never intended to do vector graphics.

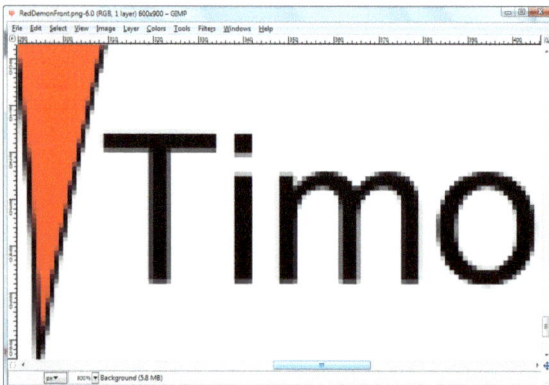

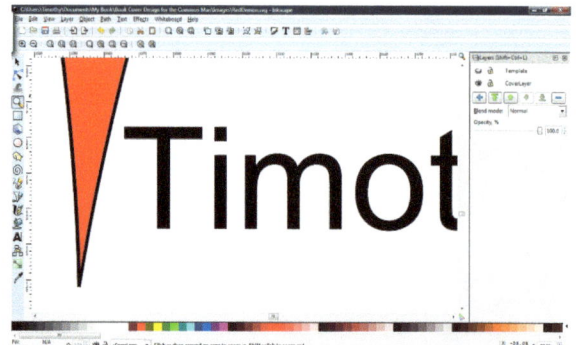

We begin to see the advantages of one over the other when we compare the result of zooming in on the same portion of the image. When we zoom into the Gimp image on the left, it loses quality, but zooming into the Inkscape image gives us sharp edges. But that's just part of the story. Though Gimp provides us with much more power than Inkscape does in terms of editing existing images, Gimp and all rastor graphics packages have the problem that once something has been painted on the image, there's no way to correct it without undoing it and starting over.

Vector graphics is a completely different way of doing things. With vector graphics, one we draw a shape on the screen, we can move it around and reshape it to our heart's content.

Though you almost don't need layers with a vector graphics program, Inkscape allows us to use layers. For this cover, I used two layers. One layer is for the cover itself and the other is for the Template. But before I did that, I set the paper size to 17x11.

To do that, select File|Document Properties from the menu.

On the Page tab, scroll down and select 11x17.

Select Landscape.

Back in the edit area, drag the Template.png file onto the screen.

The Template image will be too large for the page. To correct this, scroll out using the minus sign near the top of the window. Resize the Template image to match the page guide on the screen.

On the Layers menu, select Layers. This will display the layers to the side.

Rename the one layer there to Template.

Use the Plus sign in the Layers sidebar to add a new layer below the Template. Call it CoverLayer, or something similar. We will do all of our drawing there, so that we can hide or show the Template at any time.

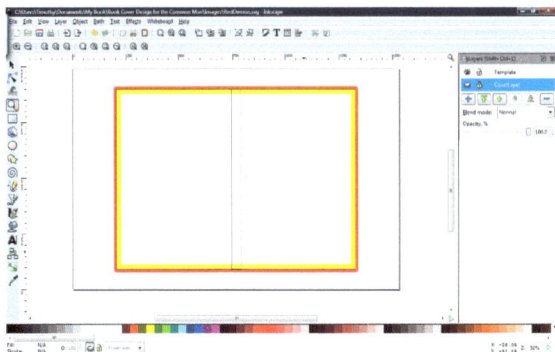

As I did with Gimp, I strongly encourage you to play with the tools that are available to you in Inkscape before you attempt to design a cover. Once you've played with them to see what they do, you'll be much more comfortable with using them as you attempt to do your work.

Some of the tools look similar to those that you've been using in Gimp. They have a similar function and operate in about the same way, but because the two tools are fundamentally different, you will find that the way a tool works in one may not match how it works in the other.

The Bucket Fill tool, for example, works differently in Inkscape than you might expect. In Gimp, the tool will fill either a selection, a layer, or everything with a similar color that is connected to a point. In Inkscape, it appears to function the same way, filling in the space between objects on the screen, but when we remove those objects, the filled area remains behind as an object in its own right. We can move it, shape it, and do everything else to it that we can do with objects we drew using other methods.

There are couple of different ways to begin drawing the red demon shape for the front of this cover. One is the Draw Freehand Lines tool ![pencil icon]. This tool works similar to the way a pencil tool works in a raster graphic program, but nodes are created along the path that you can go back and modify using the Edit Paths by Node tool ![node icon]. It will generally generate more nodes than you really need, but you can simplify the path by pressing Ctrl+L on the keyboard or selecting Simplify from the Paths menu.

As you can see from my freehand attempt at the right, there will be variations from what we intend. My attempt was done with a pen tablet. If you are using a mouse, you will have even less control. Just the act of thinking about where you want to draw next can cause your hand to become unsteady and the path will waver.

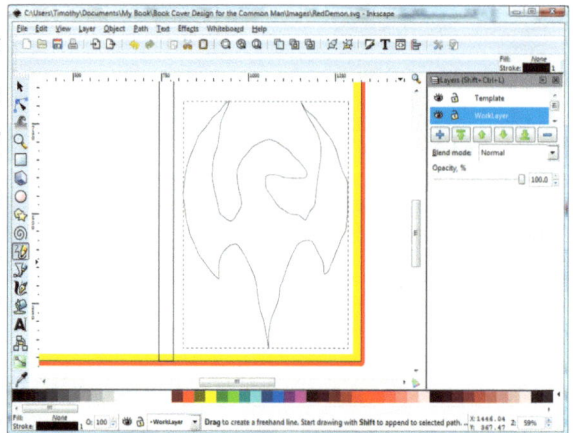

In the second image, you can see what the image looks like after we switch to the Edit Paths by Node tool ![node icon]. The reason there are so many nodes is that the tool has no way of knowing whether those variations from a nice smooth curve were intended or not. It stores them all and we have the responsibility of going back to correct our mistakes. The first thing we will do is to press Ctrl+L to simplify the drawing.

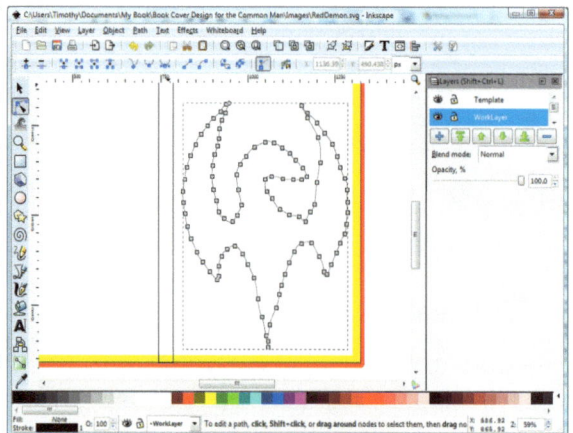

This gives us the following:

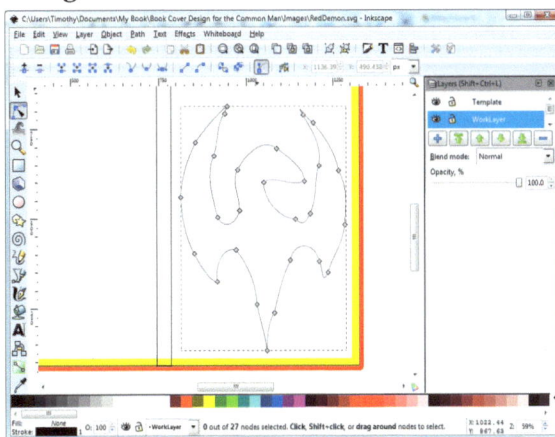

This will give us much smoother lines, but we can simplify it farther. With the Edit Paths by Node tool . Select the nodes that we don't need, one by one, and press the Delete key.

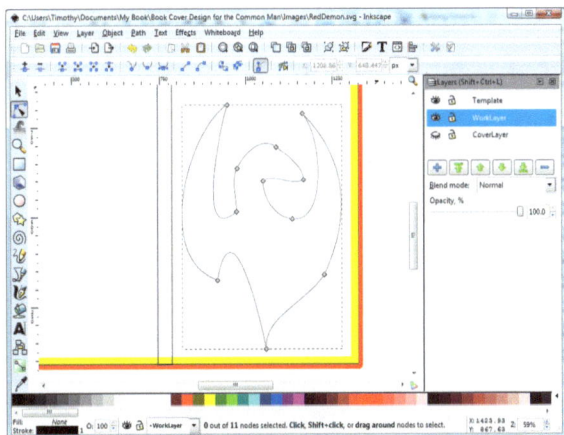

Here, I have gotten it down to eleven nodes. The lines are smooth, but it no longer looks like the image we were aiming for. We can correct that.

Still using the Edit Paths by Node tool , pull on the lines and adjust the nodes to get them into the position you want them. If need be, adjust the handles on the nodes to sharpen of smooth out the bends in the line.

After just a little work, the drawing can look like this:

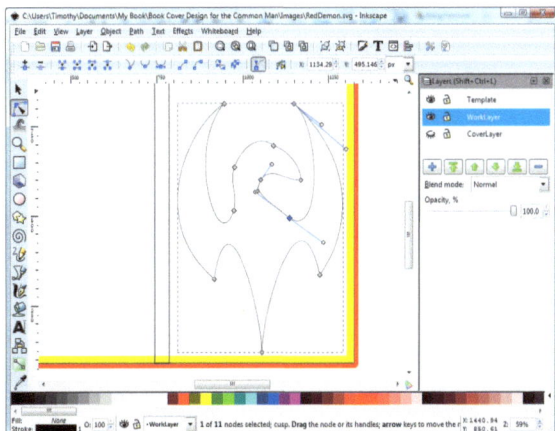

51

The only thing we need now is to fill the drawing with color. You do that by clicking on one of the colors at the bottom of the screen.

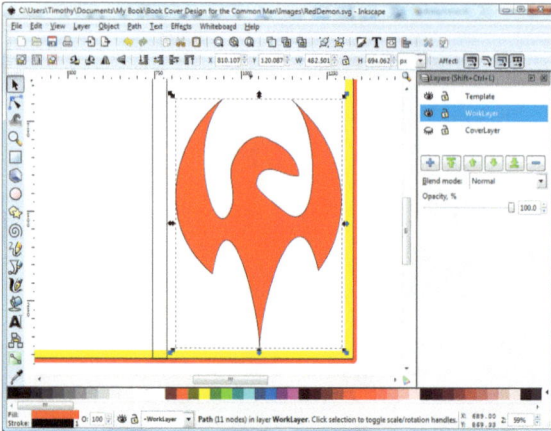

If you care to do so, Inkscape has the ability to draw much more elaborate images. For the book *Church Website Design: A step by step approach*, I used a vector graphics program to draw the spider that appears on the front cover. It is more complicated than the red demon we drew above, but even that is simple compared to some of the artwork that can be drawn.

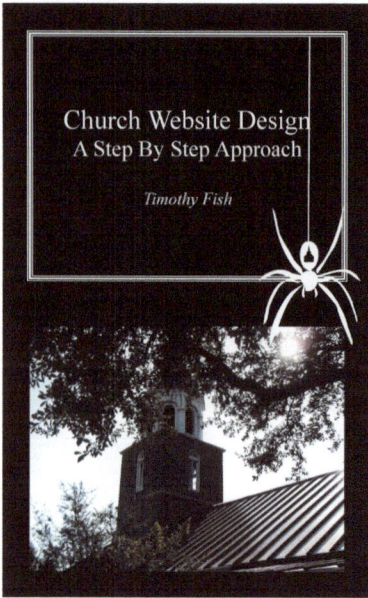

You have seen clipart that programs like Microsoft Word makes available to users. Many of these clipart files are in a vector graphics format, such as *wmf*, the file format of the image shown here. It is beyond the scope of this book to demonstrate how to draw detailed vector graphic images. Suffice it to say that with a creative mind you have a lot of power at your fingertips.

Used with permission from Microsoft.

Inkscape will allow you to save your drawings in the *emf* file format. In that format, you will be able to use the images you create like you would clipart, scaling the image to the size you need without the pixels of the image showing.

Though you may not think about it that way, most of the fonts we use are vector graphics. That is why that as we add the text as the final touches of this cover that we can resize the text to whatever size looks best without fear that that we'll begin to see the pixels of the letters. We do that with the Text tool .

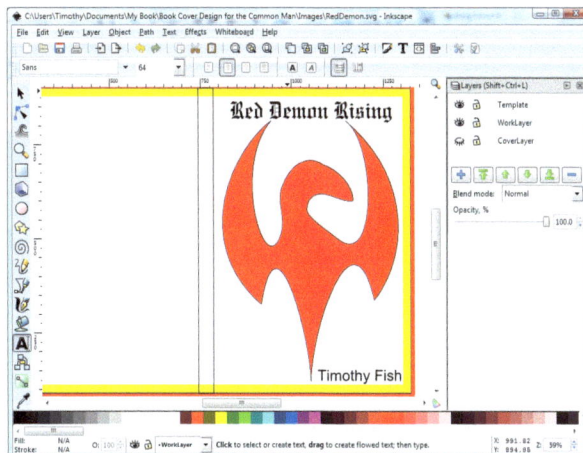

By now, I'm sure you have a good idea of how to work with text. The one thing I will note is that to change the font in Inkscape you will need to use the menu Text|Text and Font or press Ctrl+Shift+T on the keyboard. The interface on the main screen doesn't work the way you would expect.

We should also look at how to put text on the spine in Inkscape.

While in Select Mode , select the title text that you have created and copy it by pressing Ctrl+C.

Paste the text using Ctrl+V.

Drag the new text object over to the spine.

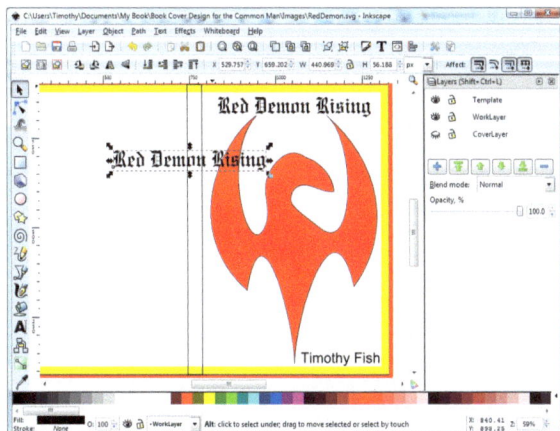

Click the Rotate 90° Clockwise button at the top of the screen.

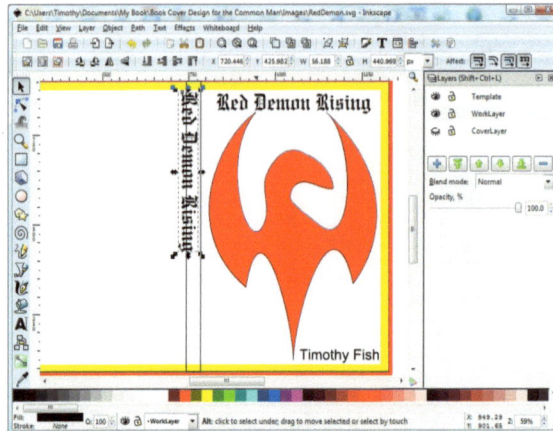

Hold down the Ctrl key and with the mouse, drag the handles of the object until it is the correct size for the spine. The Ctrl key will cause the text to resize proportionally.

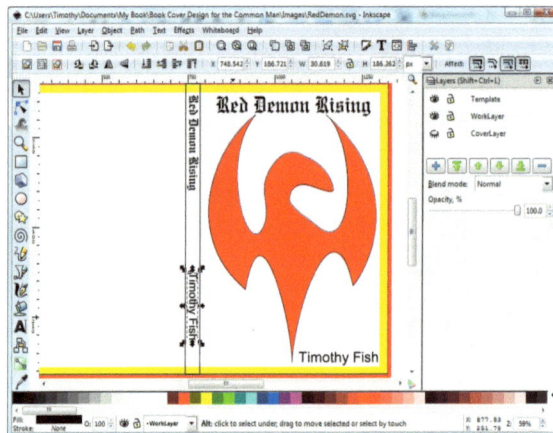

Remember to leave enough room below the author's name for your imprint logo, if you have one.

We also need to add the barcode, if we have one.

Drop the PDF file with the barcode in it onto the Inkscape window. Inkscape will take a while to process it, but it will eventually give you an import window. Click Okay.

The barcode will appear as an object on the screen.

To size the barcode to the proper size, select it and then select Object|Transform from the menu or press Ctrl+Shift+M.

On the Scale tab, check the Scale Proportionally box.

Set the width to 2 inches. The height will resize automatically. Click Apply.

Position the barcode in the bottom right of the back cover.

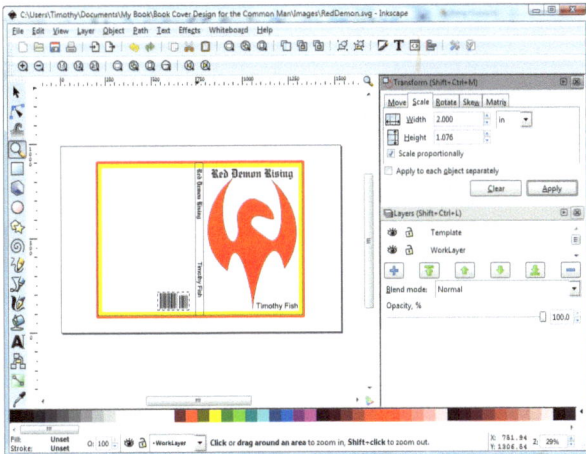

And we're done, so it is time to turn off the Template layer and convert our work to PDF for the printers. Fortunately, Inkscape has some limited capability for saving to PDF. To create our PDF file, we need only select File|Save a Copy or press Ctrl+Shift+Alt+S.

When the dialog box shown here appears, choose PDF as the output type.

Choose an appropriate name and click Save.

The PDF file will be saved in that location.

One of the nice things you will notice with the PDF file is that you can zoom all the way in and your graphics will remain sharp because Acrobat as the ability to process vector graphics.

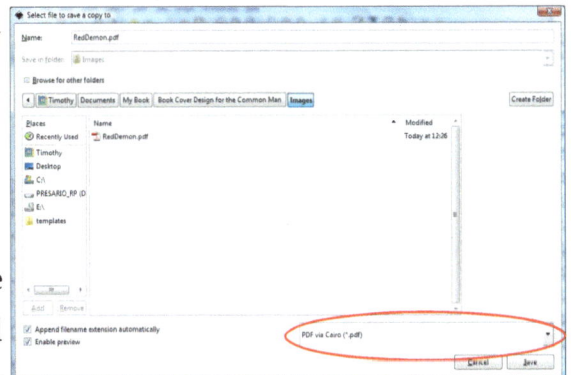

The Simple Non-fiction Cover

So far, we've spent a lot of time looking at covers for novels. We should not ignore the non-fiction cover, since many of the people reading this are considering the cover design for a non-fiction book rather than a novel.

There are a lot of similarities between non-fiction and fiction, but there are enough differences that we should give special consideration to what we hope to accomplish with a cover for a non-fiction book. That partly depends on the nature of the book, but primarily, we want the reader to be able to look at the cover and know how the book will help him. With the book you are reading, for example, we want the reader to know that it will help him design better book covers. But if the book was an algebra textbook, we would want the reader to realize that it covers the topic of algebra. With novels, we want to create an appealing image of the world of the story, but with non-fiction we want the reader to believe he will be better off after reading the book.

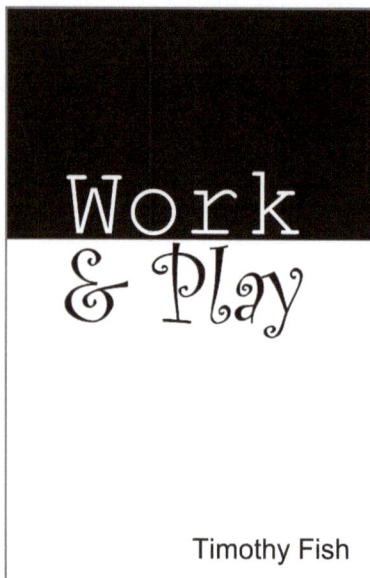

In the example shown here, we once again have about as simple of a cover as we can get. We've even limited it to black and white, but what I'd like you to notice about this cover is that we have conflict between the two words in the title. Even without a subtitle, we're able to see that the book is about the balance between work and play.

Inkscape is ideal for creating a cover like this. Everything we will draw for the cover can be drawn with very little trouble using the tools available to us in Inkscape. And once they are in place it will be easy to adjust them.

First draw a black rectangle in the top section.

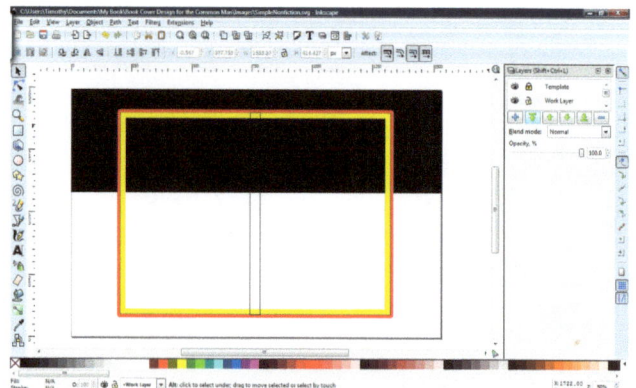

In this case, it doesn't matter so much where you draw it, but you want it to look nice. If your title has two contrasting concepts of significantly different lengths, you may need to give special thought to where you divide the two sections based on where the division will fall on the spine. For example, if the title was *Christmas Gifts & Thanksgiving Turkey*, The spine would look something like this:

To make room for the title, the author's name and the publisher information on the spine, we are forced to put the break where it is. If we were to put it closer to the center we could not separate the two sections of the title.

You have the option, if you want, to divide the spine and the front at separate locations, which would look something like this:

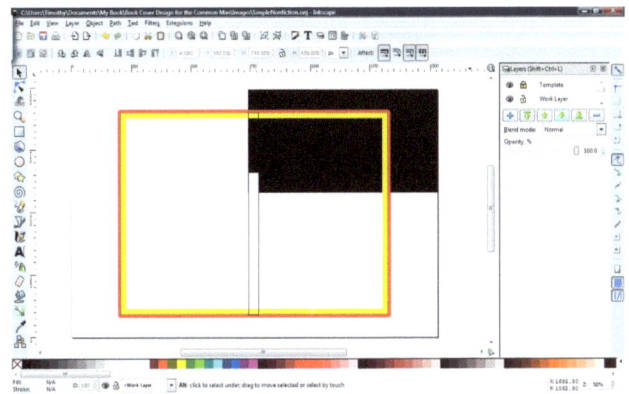

You will see the covers on some published books where the cover designer did that. I personally believe it looks sloppy. The image below represents how the book might look if you saw it lying on a table or on the floor next to a chair. While we may be tempted to think of the spine and the front separately, we often see them together. As you can see from the picture, the black area looks jagged. To add to the problem, if the cover is placed

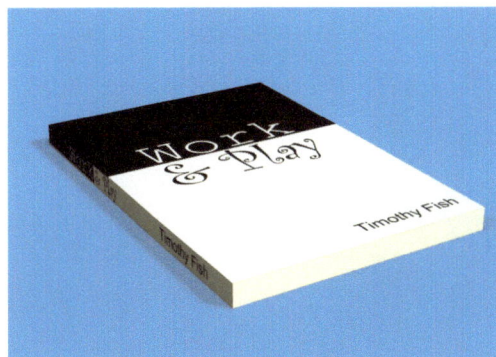

on the book just slightly off center, the corner from the spine will appear on the front of the book or part of the dividing line from the front will appear on the spine. When the book does happen to be lying in such a way that we only see one of the two, we may have an odd looking line. It is better to have the dividing line follow a straight line all the way from front edge to back edge. The result is a book that looks like this:

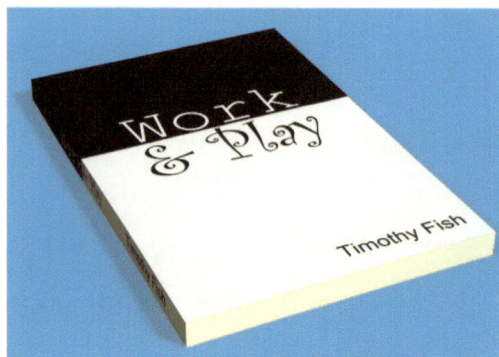

The rest of the cover design is just more of the stuff we covered earlier in this book. You need only place the text on the cover and save the to a PDF or export an image. The only thing left that is worth noting is the choice of font for the title. The difference in font is what makes it okay for us to have a cover this simple. The top font looks like what might have come from a typewriter, while the bottom font it one that looks rather playful. Even with us staying with black and white, it looks like we've given it some thought, rather than just slapping some stock photo on our book.

A book with a title this simple will probably have a subtitle of some sort. That will help our simple cover. In the image below, we see the cover with the subtitle added. The design is just as simple as before, but the additional text fills in part of the empty spaces, giving the book a more finished look.. The subtitle is non intrusive and most people won't remember that it is there. With a cover like this, there is plenty of room to add more text and people will remember only that title is set up the way it is.

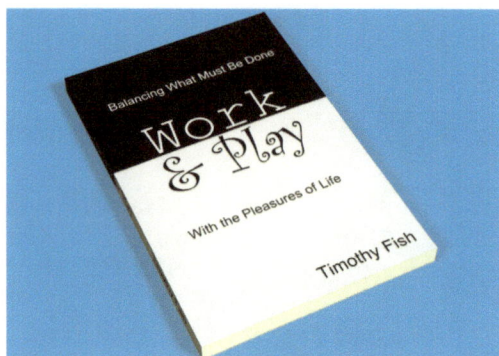

More You Can Do With Text

If you've looked at some of the books in bookstores, you know that there is a lot that you can do with text. Some text is raised or lowered. Some is metallic gold or silver. Some is shiny. Some is flat. You could even have the text cut out, so that people can see what is behind the cover. But while that is possible, it isn't likely that the self-publishing author will have the opportunity to design a cover that way. If you are designing for POD, you will most likely be limited to whatever will fit on an 17x11 sheet of paper or at most an 18x12 sheet of paper. The machine will print the color image, laminate one side and slap it on the book. It is easier to put all that fancy text on a book printed with offset printing because the pages of the book are printed separately from the cover. Sometimes, two separate companies will print them.

But don't despair, there is still much we can do with text. In fact, since many people will be viewing the covers online, it is possible to create a cover that looks just like those of the offset printed books. Gimp has a number of filters preinstalled that allow us to convert text into interesting shapes and colors. The following is the frosty Alpha to Logo filter:

Because it uses a script, all you have to do to produce something like that is to create a text layer and select the filter from the filters menu. It's far from a complete cover, but it

demonstrates the power available to you in Gimp.

To achieve a similar result, first use the Text tool to create text in an image.

I used the Rockwell Bold font at 18pt for this example. The image size I used is 900x600 pixels. For the Frosty filter, you need enough

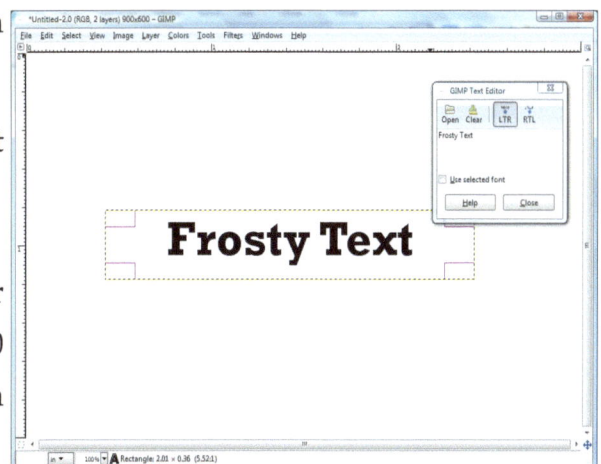

space around the text for it to draw. With all of these filters, larger works better.

Select the filter from Filter | Alpha to Logo | Frosty while you have the text layer active.

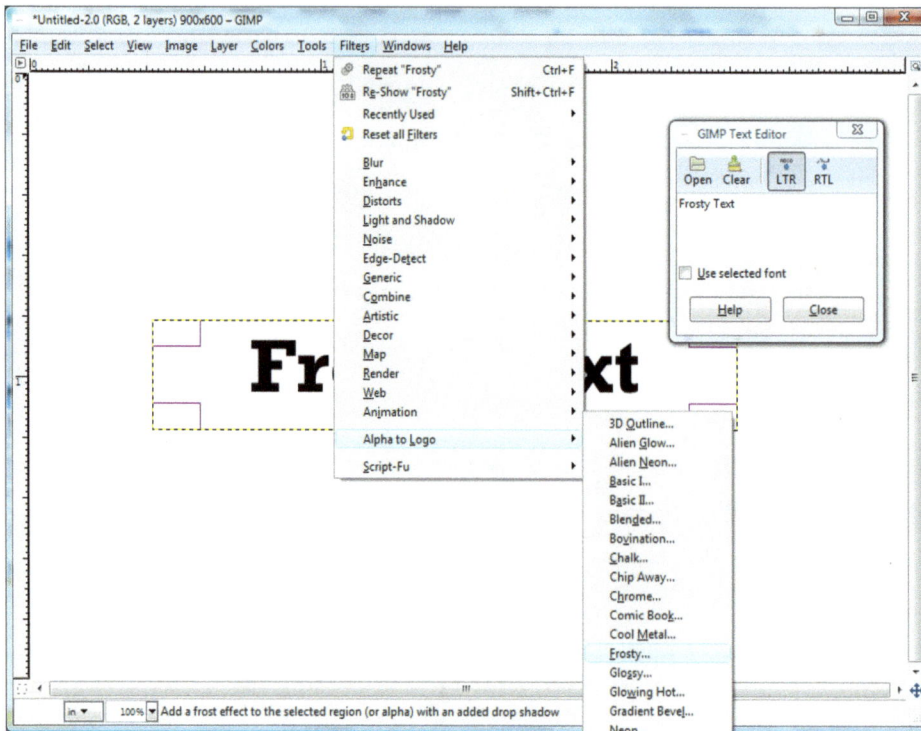

You will see a dialog box like the following:

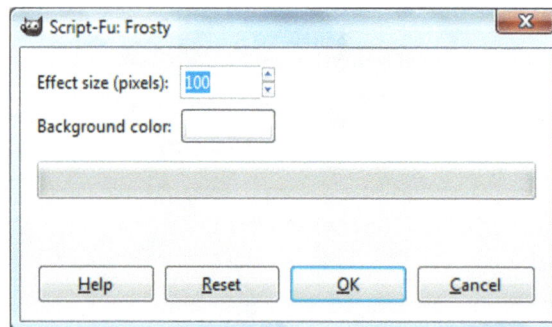

If you look at the top of this dialog box you will see that it says "Script-Fu: Frosty". Script-Fu is Gimp's terminology for scripts and Frosty is just an add-on script that someone wrote for the basic Gimp package. It is outside the scope of this book, but if you find you are doing some tasks in Gimp frequently or there is an effect you would like to apply again, you can create your own scripts.

As far as I can tell, the Background Color setting does nothing. The Effect Size, however, impacts various things. It is worth your time to play with the filter to see what results you get with different Effect Sizes. Here are some examples:

Effect Size 50

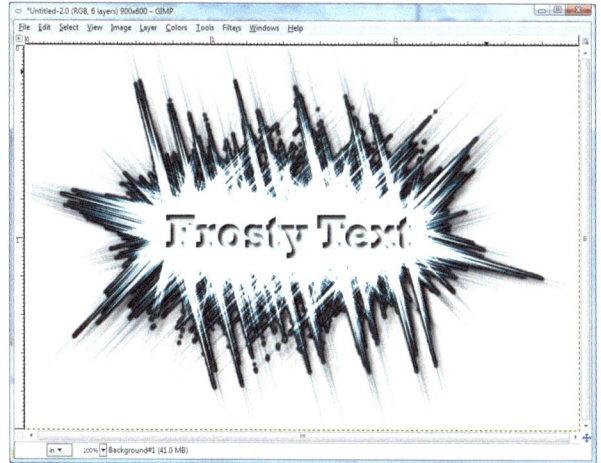

Effect Size 100

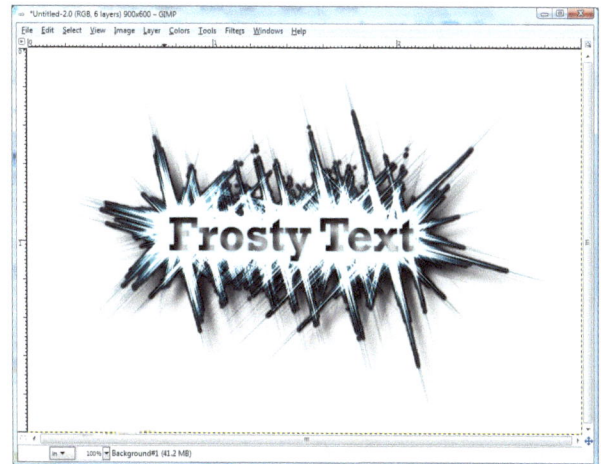

Effect Size 200

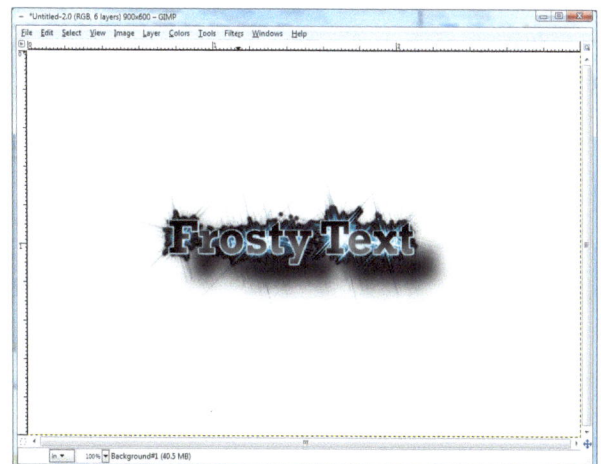

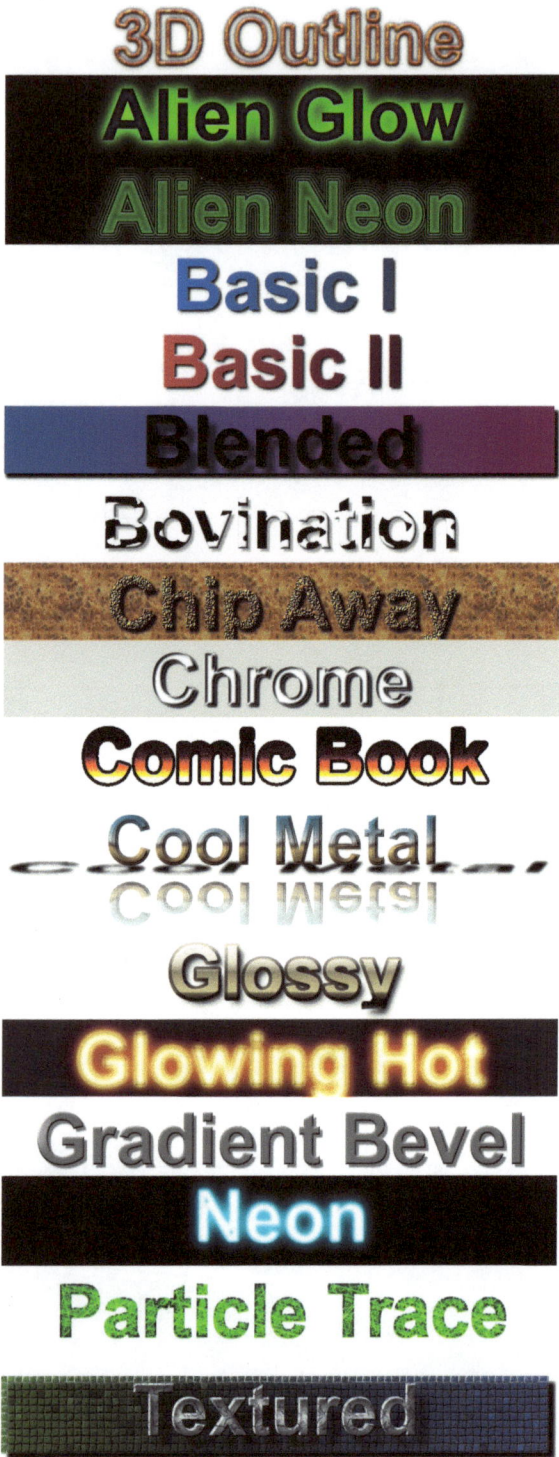

I know it looks like I messed up the labels, but that is not the case. A smaller effect size gives you a larger effect when using this filter. What you should take from that is that by playing with a script you may discover things you didn't expect.

On the left are the various filters applied using the default settings. There is some potential there and it is easy enough to apply them to text on our covers, but the danger we run into is the temptation to grab one of these styles slap it on the cover and call it good.

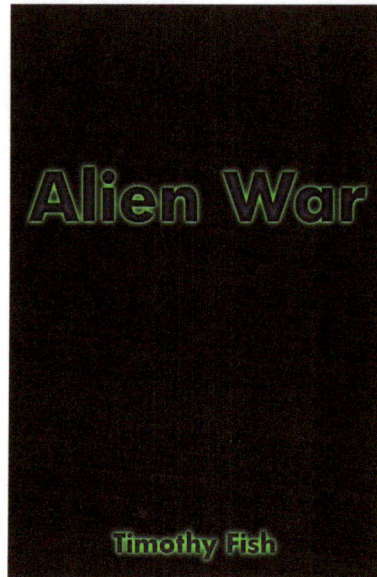

Here is one example. While it might work fine for a cover, it is useful for us to question whether we want our book too look like what other people could just as easily produce by opening Gimp, entering some text and applying a filter.

At the very least, we need to pay special attention to the placement of the text on the cover. Compare the cover you see above with similar covers shown below.

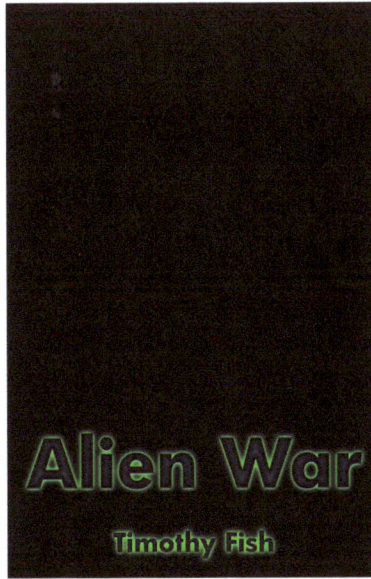

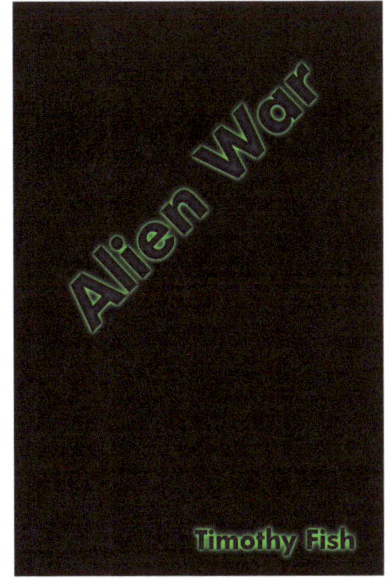

Notice how different these covers look and yet the only difference is in the text placement. But these built-in filters really come into their own when they are used with text that goes with a matching image. You may recognize the face below as the same face we used on one of the earlier covers, but here we've desaturated the color of the face and used a green (the same green as is in the text) layer above it to multiply those colors.

Usually, when we apply text to an image we choose colors that make it appear that we've applied ink to the surface, but one of the things we can do with text is to apply it in such a way that it appears there is no ink and the surface itself is formed in the shape of the letters. Look at this example cover. While it is too simple to use on a real book, there are several things that are worth discussing for their potential use on other covers.

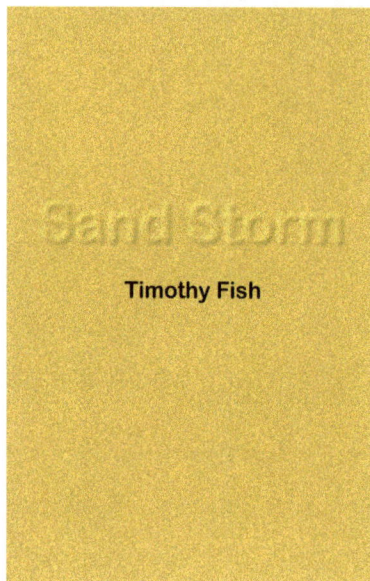

In keeping with the theme of this section of the book, the focus of the cover is on the text. What we hope to accomplish with this design is to give the cover the appearance of the words being covered with sand, but the wind had blown enough away that we can tell what it says.

The first thing we need is sand. If you have a picture of sand, you could used that, but in this case, we want to let Gimp produce the sand for us.

Start with the usual template and a layer that is completely white. With the white layer active apply the HSV Noise filter by selecting Filters|Noise|HSV Noise, as is show here.

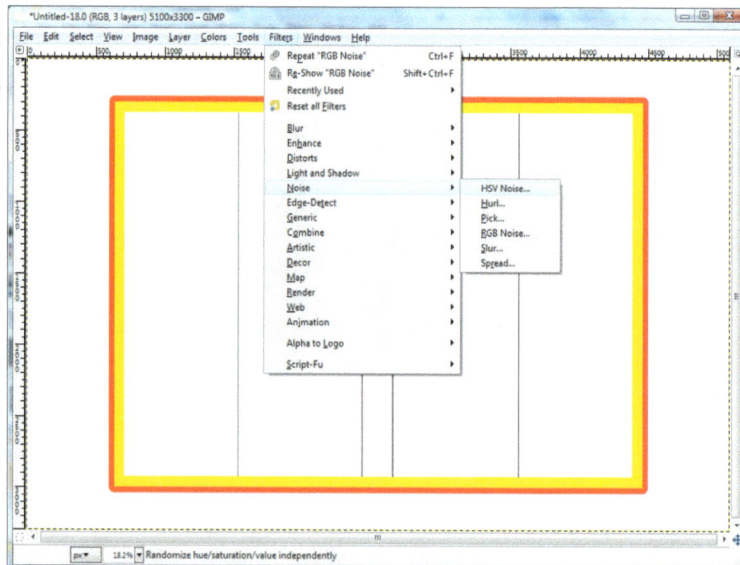

This should bring up the HSV Noise dialog box. The values you choose aren't particularly important because we're just trying to get some random noise, but we do want to set the Saturation at 0 so that we don't have to do the extra step of desaturating the result after we've produced the noise.

The preview pane gives us an idea of what the result will be. As you can see, it already looks a little like sand, but it is too dark in some places and too light in others. It doesn't have the tan color that we had with the example book cover.

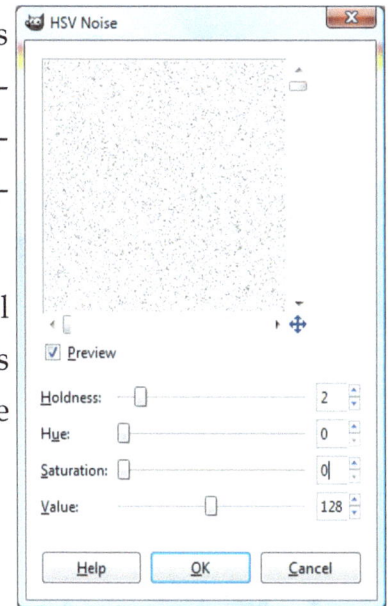

Click Ok.

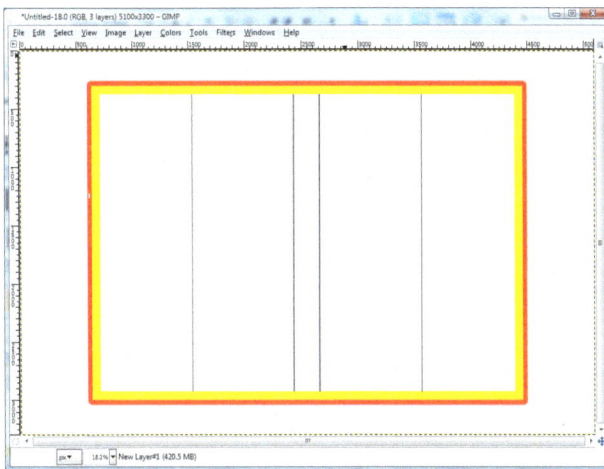

The resulting image looks like the image above. At this level of magnification, it looks more like gray than sand, but if we zoom in it looks more like what we would expect.

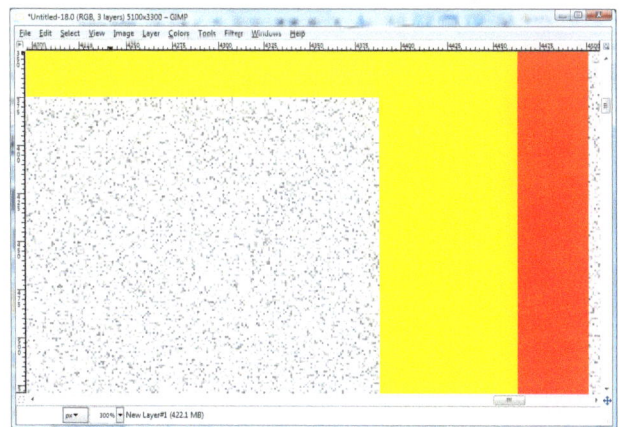

It is also too light for what we want to do to it. All of that white will mess us up, so we need to invert the colors. To do that, select Colors|Invert.

The result will give us something much darker.

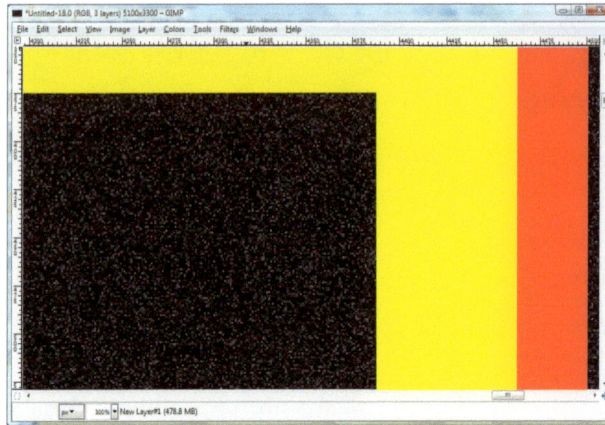

Create a new layer above the noise layer and fill it with the color having HTML notation "ffd870".

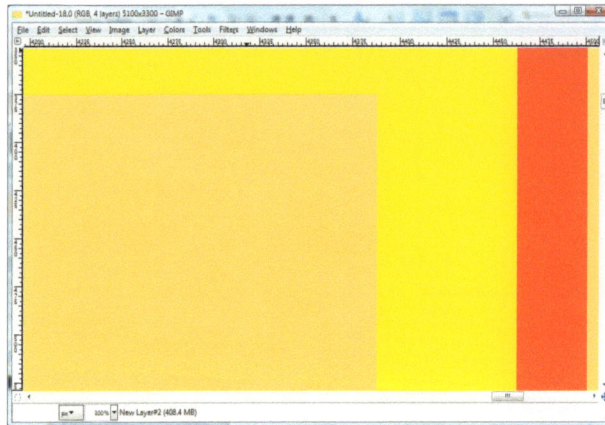

Set the Mode of the new layer to Difference.

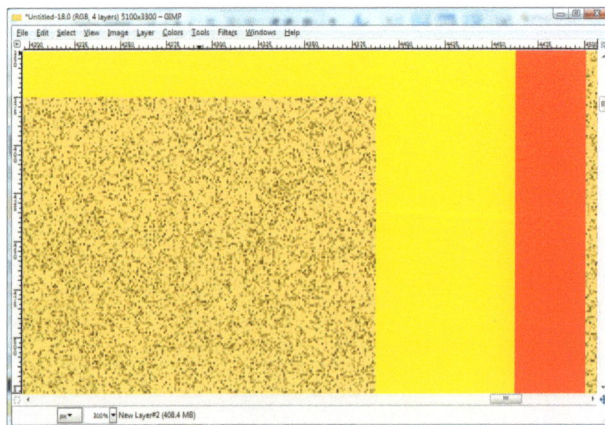

As you can see, all of the darkest area of the underlying layer are now tan and the lightest areas are darker. This is because the numeric values of the dark areas were near zero and the light areas were higher.

Here is what it looks like when we move back out to 100%.

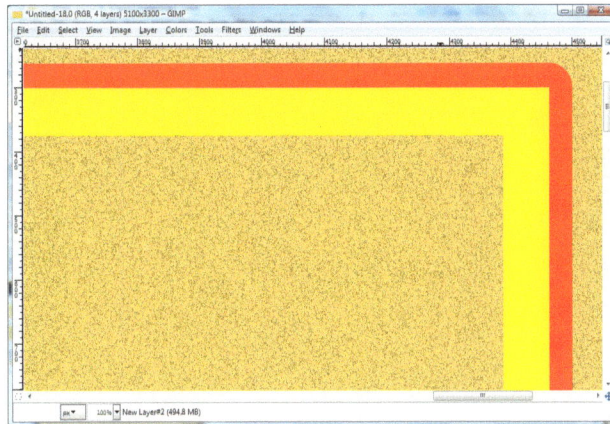

When we begin to consider how to shape our sand into the raised letters of the title, we are moving ever so slightly away from the two dimensional world into the three dimensional world. Imagine, if you will that you have a drawing—perhaps like the one shown here. In the two dimensional world, we are only concerned with where the stars are placed in two directions. But suppose we were to lay that image down and we wanted to reposition those stars in such a way that they were not on the paper but are some distance away from the paper. To do that, we need a way to specify the distance away from the paper.

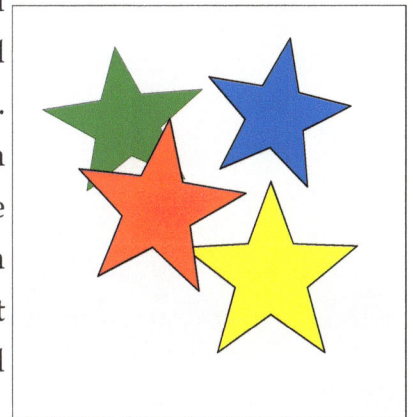

In a true three dimensional drawing we work with X, Y and Z. Whereas in a two dimensional drawing we have only X and Y. The problem Gimp has is that it is a two dimensional drawing tool and we come along and want to tell it to draw something based on that third dimension. We need to be able to tell it what part of our image is raised and what isn't. To do that, we use the values

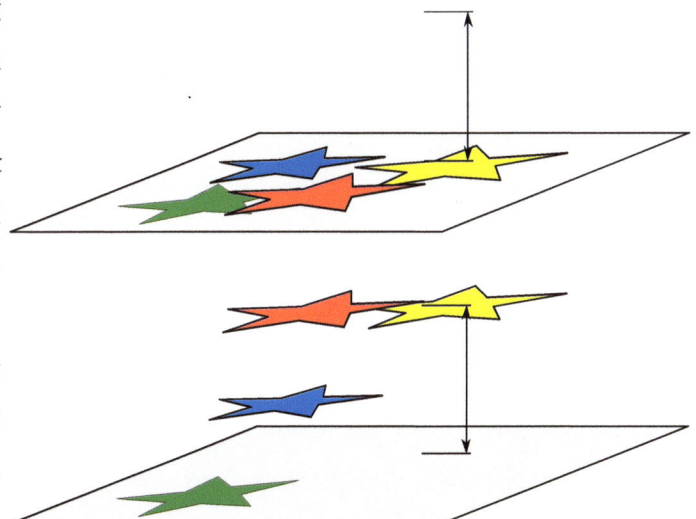

in the drawing as that third dimension. We're somewhat limited because we have only 256 values along that axis, but it will work for our purpose. If we need more than that, we can move over into a truly three dimensional drawing tool.

With Black being equal to zero and white being the value of the height we determined for the yellow star, our values along the Z-axis would look something like the image show here. This image was created in Gimp by selecting each star and filling it with a shade of gray using the Paint Bucket. The green star will not appear in this image because its height is the same as the paper.

While it isn't as impressive as one might hope based on what we saw in the previous page, this next image is what the Gimp produces when we apply the gray stars to a white layer as a Bump Map. This problem goes back to the problem of us only being able to look at the image as if we were above it. The fact that we can see anything at all is because Gimp used antialiasing to soften the edges of the stars at some point.

As you can expect, we'll have the same problem with our text. It's easy enough to create our text; we've done it often enough. For this we'll need white text, since we want it to look like the text is raised. I used Arial Rounded.

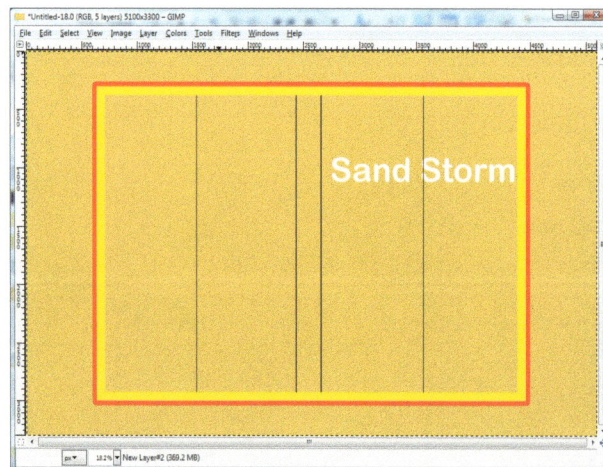

It's okay to leave the text with the transparent background. When we apply the Bump Map, Gimp knows what to do with the transparent part of the layer.

We can also click the eye ◉ on the Text layer to hide it. We don't want to see the white in our image, but we do want to use the layer.

To apply the text as a Bump Map, first click on the Tan Colored layer to activate it. Then select from the menus Filters|Map|Bump Map. This will bring up the Bump Map Dialog box.

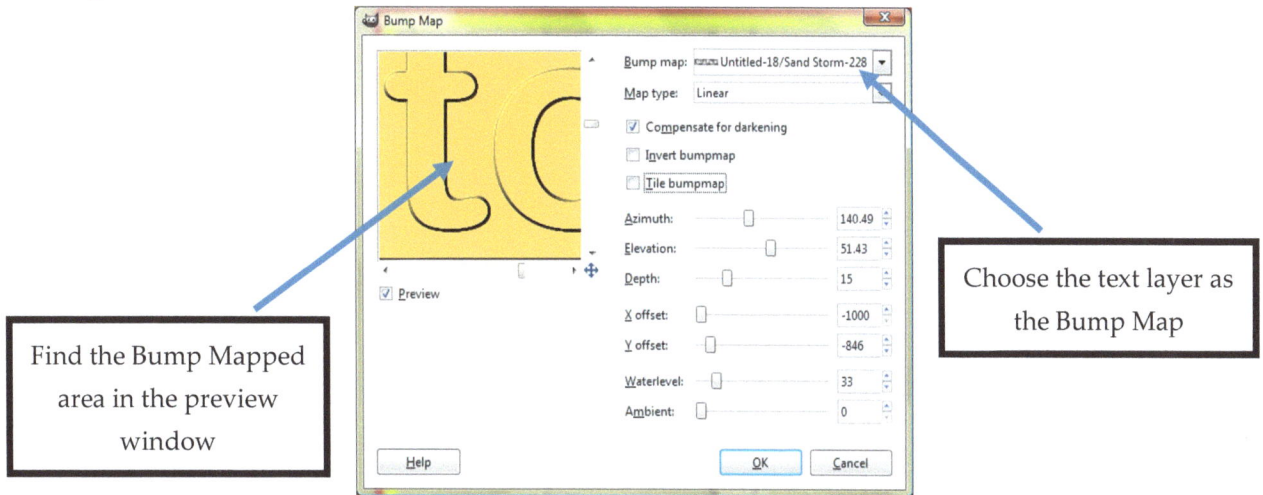

Find the Bump Mapped area in the preview window

Choose the text layer as the Bump Map

As always, play with the settings to see what results you get. You may have to do a little searching for the text in the preview window, since the image we're working with is large and the text is in a small area of it. When you're satisfied with the result, click Ok.

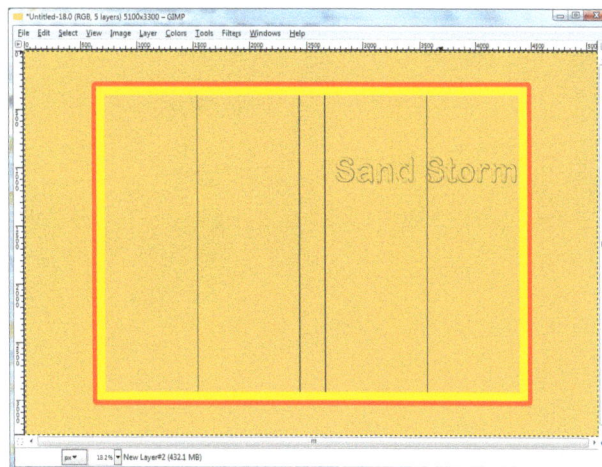

As you can see from this image, the result is very similar to what we saw with the stars. There's enough there for us to see the outline of the letters, but it doesn't look anything like the letters are formed from sand.

It isn't what we want, so undo what we just did by pressing Ctrl+Z.

To correct the problem, we need to modify our text layer so that the Bump Map doesn't make all of each letter the same height. We need the outer edge of the letters to be close to the paper and the middle to be higher.

The easiest way to accomplish that is to blur the text. With the text layer active and visible, select Filters | Blur | Gaussian Blur from the menus.

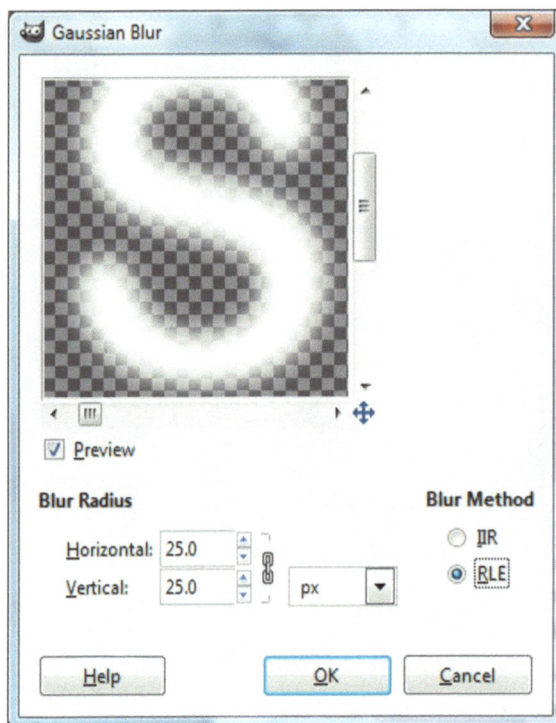

Set the Horizontal and Vertical blue radiuses to 25 pixels and click Ok. This will cause a smooth transition from white to transparent around the edges of the letters.

Now, repeat the process of applying the Bump Map, this time with the blurred text as the map.

Symbols and Old Books

You will recall that the prop book for *The Neverending Story* movie was leather-bound and had a symbol on the front with two intertwined snakes eating each other, tail first. We won't reproduce that cover design, for a number of reasons. For one thing, the symbol itself isn't likely to be one that will fit any story other than *The Neverending Story*. Another reason is that we are limited to producing books with paper or hardback covers. And yet another reason is that the prop was 11x14.5 inches and about two inches thick.

There was a time when it made sense to make books like that. Books were expensive. Each page had to be copied by hand, taking many hours to do the work. Once the pages were completed, they were bound in leather because leather would hold up to many years of use. Anyone who owned a book would want to be able to show it off, so the book makers would add decorative elements. Because some books were so very expensive, it was a relatively low cost to apply metal artwork to the cover.

These days, the cost of printing a book is so low that people aren't as willing to pay for artwork on the book. Our covers today are primarily to tell people what the book is about, whereas the old books were so rare that educated people generally knew that they were about but needed a means of protecting the book. Today, you will only see a person buying a book like that if they are a fan of the book and have a desire to own an attractive copy to show off. You might, for example, find a replica of *The Neverending Story* prop in someone's living room with the text of the book inside.

While we can't expect someone to pay hundreds of dollars for our book just because it looks like an old book, it is appropriate to give some books the appearance of being old. In stories like *The Neverending Story*, there is an old book that plays a key role in the story. Even though the book the reader holds is probably paperback, if the reader is able to turn

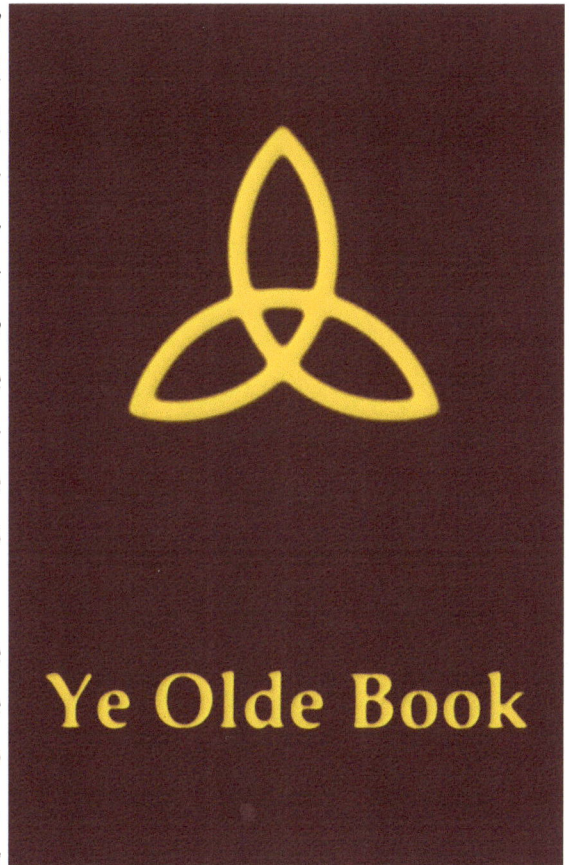

the book over and see the same cover as what the book in the story has it adds to the reader involvement in the story.

The technique for applying a medallion to the cover is similar to the technique we used in the last section to raise text in the sand. The major difference in this section is that we want to separate the images from the background.

We need a symbol to place on the front of the book. The one shown here will do fine as an example. It is the most basic of the Celtic knots and requires the least effort to draw because it is formed by the arcs of three circles. While this design is attractive in its own right, you can search the web for Celtic knots and see much more elaborate knots that will also work well for a medallion.

To draw this in Gimp, we first use the Eclipse Select tool to select a circle by using the mouse to select an area and then adjusting the width and height of that area to be the same. The placement of the circle isn't important right now.

Next, select the border of the image by choosing Select|Border from the menus. Use a width of about 30 pixels. Invert the selection and delete the unneeded white.

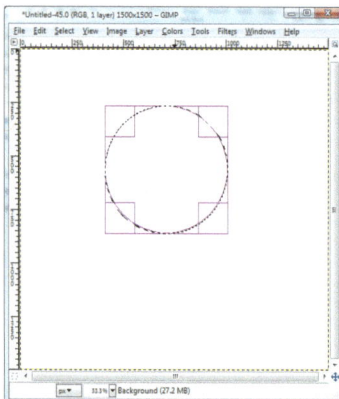

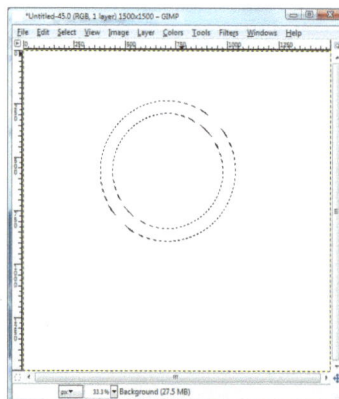

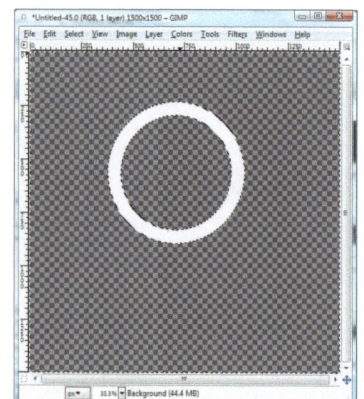

Use the duplicate layers button to duplicate the layer twice, giving you three circles.

Use the Move Tool to rearrange them to where they look like the image below.

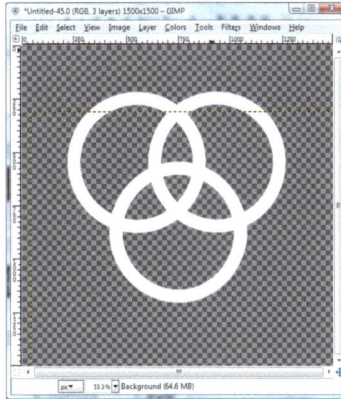

Next, we need to erase the portions of the circles that we don't need, without erasing anything we do.

To do that, use the Fuzzy Select tool to select one of the circles.

Activate a different layer, hold down the Shift key and use the Fuzzy Select tool to add the second circle to the selection.

Invert the selection. (Select|Invert)

Activate the third layer and use the Eraser tool to remove the part of the circle you don't need. Because they aren't selected, you will be able to go right up to the other circles without fear of erasing more than you should.

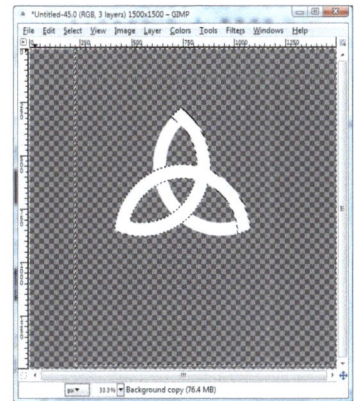

Repeat the process for the other two circles.

Now that we have the shape, we need only Select|None then Edit|Copy Visible and Paste the shape as a new layer into our book cover design.

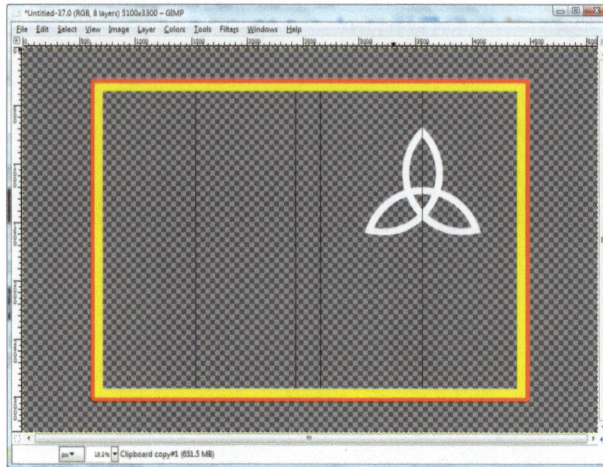

As you might expect, the first thing we're going to do with our symbol is to apply a Gaussian Blur to it.

Here is the result of a 50 pixel Gaussian Blur.

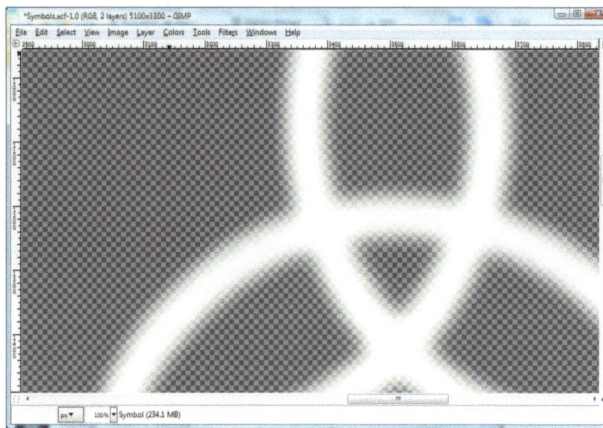

We will also be applying this to a layer as a Bump Map. For that, we need a layer that has a yellowish gold color to it. The color with HTML notation "fec900" will work nicely.

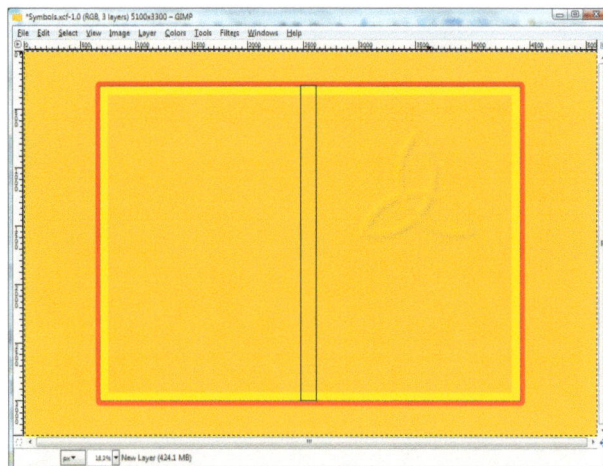

The trick now is to remove everything but the symbol from the golden layer.

Right click on the layer and select Add Layer Mask.

Choose the Black Layer option.

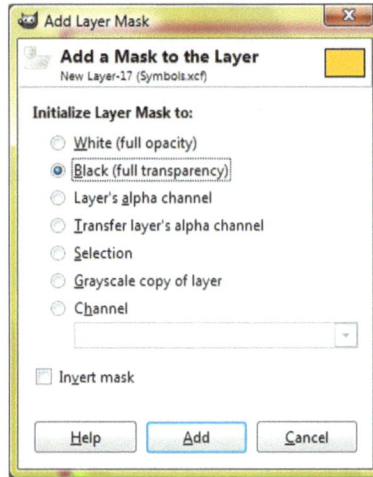

Everything on the golden layer will disappear as soon as you click Add.

Select the layer with the symbol on it and press Ctrl-C to copy the symbol.

Click the black rectangle on the golden layer and press Ctrl-V to paste the symbol into the Layer Mask.

Click the anchor to anchor the floating image.

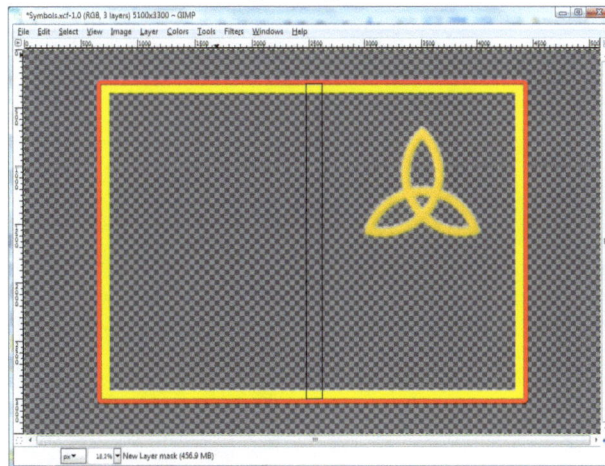

Even from this vantage point, the symbol doesn't look quite right, but we'll have an easier time seeing what we've got if we have a contrasting color behind it. Create a colored layer under the symbol with HTML notation "5e1408" and hide the white symbol by clicking the eye button on that layer.

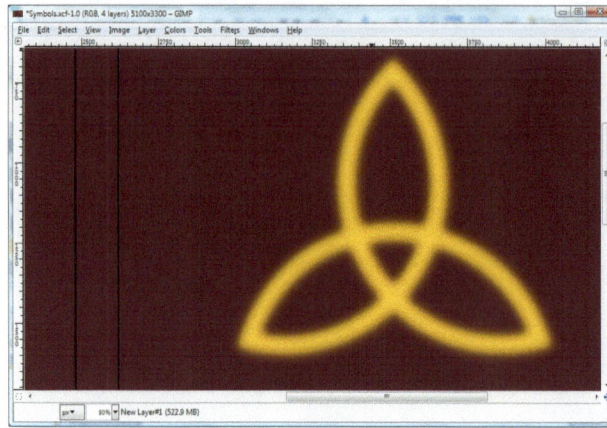

The symbol shows up clearly against the background, but it still has a fuzzy look to it, giving us the feeling that we're looking at it without the aid of our eyeglasses.

Select the Layer Mask of the golden layer.

Select Colors|Levels from the menus.

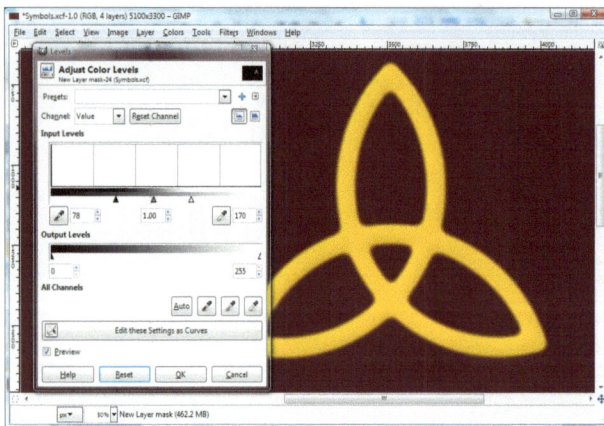

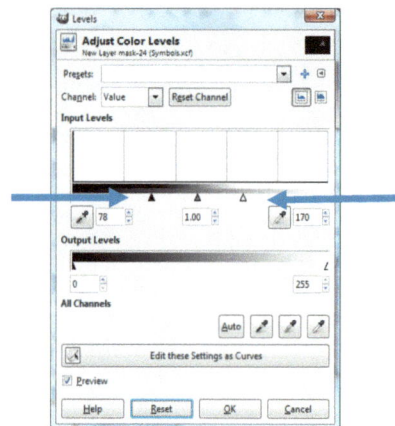

Adjust the color level of the Layer Mask by pushing the black triangle and the white triangle toward the center. You will notice the sharpness of the symbol increasing as you do. Position the triangles where you like the sharpness of the symbol.

Repeat the process with a text layer to get similar results. Replace the dark brown with a leather texture to complete the old style look.

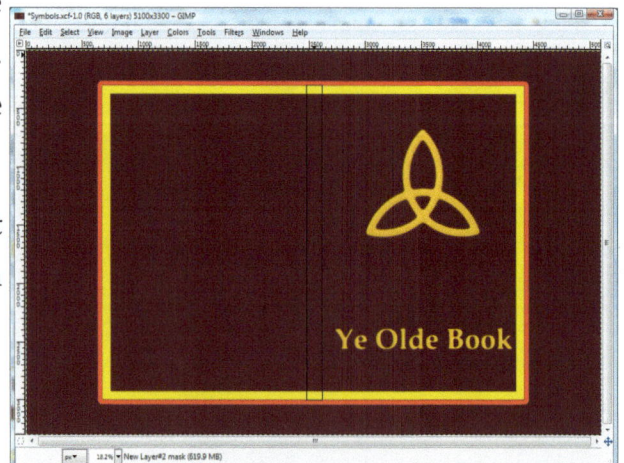

It's All About the Dress

You typically see this with romance novels, but there is a whole class of covers in which the cover model's head has been chopped off and all you can see in the foreground is the dress she is wearing. Often, it is a fancy dress that looks very expensive with many

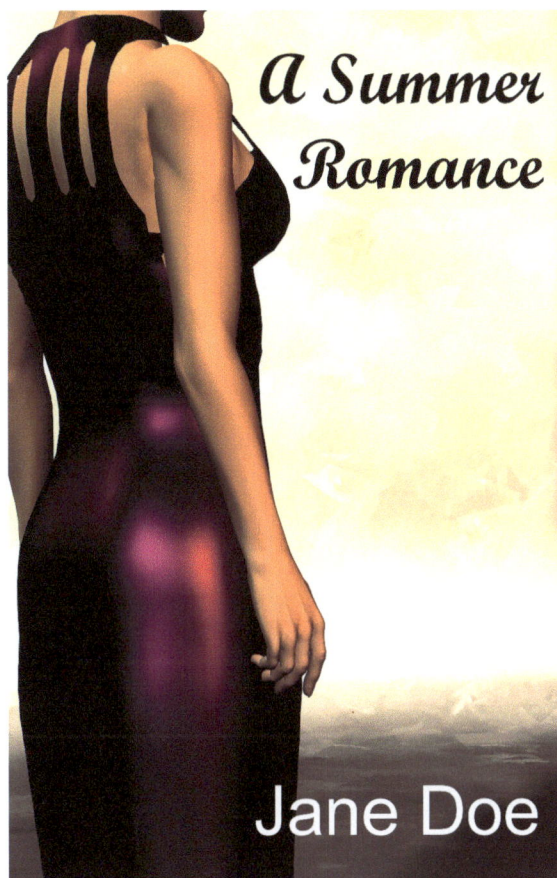

yards of fabric, but there are also instances in which the dress isn't particularly fancy, though it may tell us much about the character. If you are designing a cover for a romance novel, you may want to try this technique.

There really isn't much to say about how to accomplish a cover design like this. It really is just a photo with some text over it. If you have followed the examples so far, adding text to an image should be a very simple task. Of greater interest to us here are the choices we can make concerning the images we choose for the cover.

The choices you have may be limited by the kind of dress involved. If you're looking to include a very elaborate dress on the cover, you may have to either buy or borrow a dress that fits the description. That usually isn't a very attractive prospect for those of us who are attempting to publish a book on a shoestring. The other option is to see what you can find in the way of stock photos. Stock photos are expensive too, but it's cheaper than buying a ball gown. You'll have to work within any limitations you have, but for this discussion we'll tend to ignore those limitations for the sake of better understanding.

One of the easiest things for us to mess with using the tools we have is the positioning of the dress on the cover.

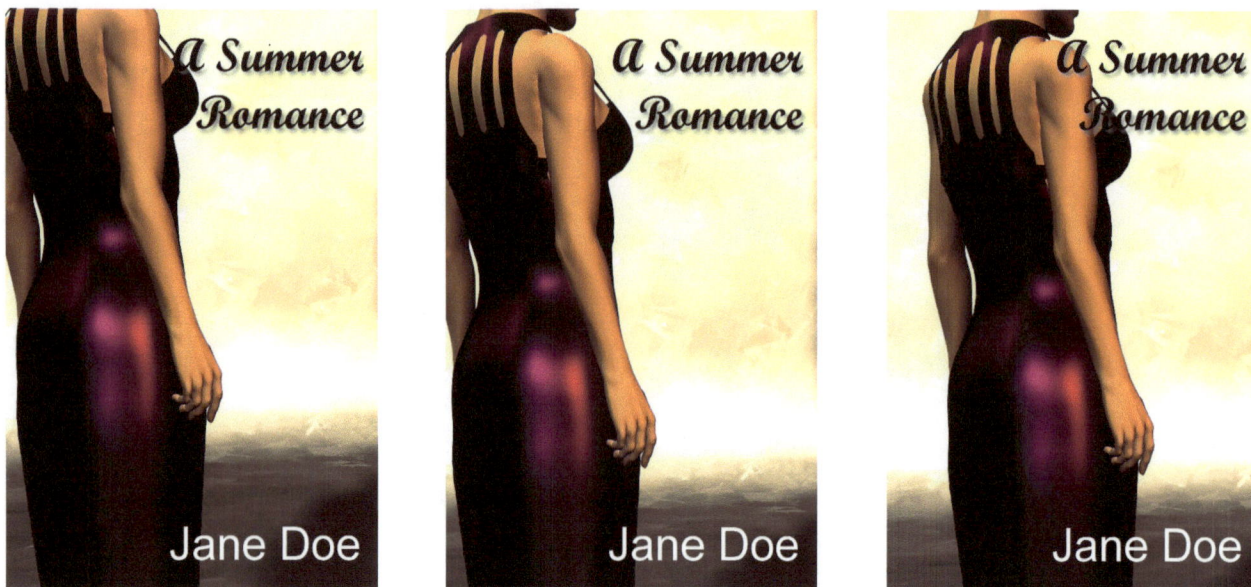

Notice how that in the first two of these images the positioning gives way to whatever is in the background. We have plenty of room back there to put whatever we want, such as the woman's future husband, a puppy dog, or whatever. The left image demonstrates that affect the most. We've not only obscured the woman's face, we've completely hidden her head and have cut into the top of the dress as well. Our eye sees the dress and the woman, but our natural tendency is to avoid focusing on that area of the picture and look toward the background. In this case, it is only a textured wall, but our eye goes there anyway.

The center image retains part of that affect, but it slows the progression. It isn't as uncomfortable to focus on the dress, but with her pushed over to the side like that, we still look toward the background, expecting something to be there. This may, in part, be due to the fact that she is also looking in that direction. The natural flow for our eye is to see where she is looking and to look in that same direction.

In the right image, we've put the dress front and center, or very close to it. It is clear to anyone who looks at this image that we intended for them to focus their attention on the dress. The head is gone, so we aren't asking people to look at the face. All the interesting parts of the dress are clearly visible. When placement like this is used, we need not worry much about what goes in the background. A simple background will do because people won't remember what is there anyway. Everyone will be looking at the dress.

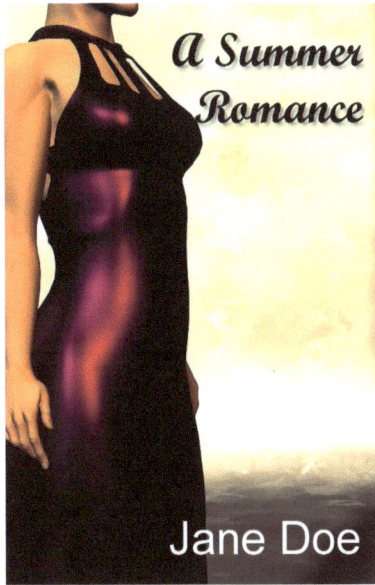

Let's turn the woman around.

Using the same placement as before, the right image has a similar affect to what we had before. The dress is front and center, so our eye is drawn to it. But the other two images have a different affect. Before, we looked at how they draw our eye from the foreground to the background. With the model turned around, we don't have the same draw. While it isn't uncomfortable to look at the background, in all of these images the natural pull is toward the dress, rather than away from it.

It's a little easier to understand when we look at this next image. Here the woman is standing at the edge of the cover as if she is about to walk out of view, but our eye is drawn toward the background. Generally, when working with people in image composition we want the characters to have look space. We want people viewing the image to be able to see something in the direction the person is looking. The difference

here is that we aren't dealing with the woman's eyes. Instead, we have a dress. Without the face attached, our minds don't process the image the same way. Without the face, it doesn't bother us that we can't see what she sees. Instead, our eye follows the natural lines of the image and we are pulled toward the background. It is almost as if we want to know what the woman is fleeing, rather than what she is heading toward.

The color of the dress can change the mood of the cover significantly. Black always gives it a formal appearance. Red stands out, drawing our attention to it. Blue and tan are toned down. The blue gives it a cool feel. The tan gives it a bright cheeriness. And white looks like we're ready for a wedding, even on the simplest of dresses.

While it may not seem right to judge people by the clothes they wear, people do it anyway. The dress that the woman on the front cover is wearing will tell people something about who the woman is. It is important that the dress accurately reflect who the person in the story is. So, in looking at colors, we might ask ourselves, is the woman in the story the type of person who would wear a red dress? Is she the type of person who would wear a blue dress? Almost any woman will willingly wear a white dress on her wedding day, but are the events of the story such that putting her in a white dress is appropriate? Is there something in the story that would cause us to believe she should be wearing a wedding dress?

Take a look at the images below. The three covers are identical, except for the dress. Take a moment to think about what each cover is telling you about the woman in the story.

The first dress looks like something a woman might wear if she didn't want to be too concerned about children getting their hands on it. This might be the dress of a mother or a teacher. The uniform in the second image has one purpose. A young woman will wear an outfit like this when she's cheering for the team, but that's about it. The third dress is one that might be worn by a more fashion conscious woman. She isn't looking for a dress

that she can take off and throw in the wash when her child gets chocolate on it, or when the dog gets his paws on it. She has no intention of ever letting that happen.

We know that in real life a woman might own all of these outfits and wear them on different occasions. The yellow dress might be what she wears when she is running around town with her girlfriends, the uniform might be what she wears to the game and the last dress might be for an evening out with her boyfriend. But in storybook world we aren't looking through her closet, we're trying to figure out what outfit we'll find her wearing in the story.

If the romance takes place while she's on vacation, we might find her in the yellow dress. If the romance takes place while a young woman is at cheerleading camp, then the second outfit will do. If we're talking about an office romance then the last outfit will do.

All in the Family

Congratulations! You have just finished your first book about your fondest memories of your father. You know better than to expect that people outside your local community will buy it, but your father was a leader in the community and you think several people will buy the book if you self-publish it. You announce your intention at a family gathering and all of your family tells you how good it is that you are recording your memories for posterity. They ask you how the book is coming and you tell them that it is complete except you need a cover for it. Most of your family just kind of nods, but your daughter speaks up and says, "Billy's good at drawing. Wouldn't be great if one of Grandpa's great grandchildren drew the cover for the book?"

Perhaps the rest of the family agrees or maybe not, but you're trapped. You don't want to say that Little Billy can't draw. He's your grandson, so of course you want to encourage his talent, but after he finishes drawing your cover, you have an image that looks like this.

I'm convinced that every family has a Little Billy. Someday, he may be a great artist. Someday, he may understand what it takes to design a cover, but today he is just a kid with some natural talent with a pencil. All Little Billys produce drawings like the one above, though some use colored pencils or crayons to do their work. Some may have graduated to watercolors or pastels or even acrylic or oil. Whatever method they use, it is unlikely that Little Billy's artwork will look great as a cover for a book.

Obviously, there is a reason why I waited this long to cover this topic. Using a pencil drawing or a painting for a book cover is not something you should be doing. I realize there are some exceptions. Some artists are so skilled with a pencil, a pen or a brush that they can produce the quality of images we would like to see on a book. The problem is that the budding young artist in you family is not likely to be that skilled. Give him a few years. Wait until he's completed the art classes in high school and has gone to college to study art, then ask him to create a cover for you and he'll give you something worth using, but until then it will be less than ideal.

You may be thinking that no one would even consider putting Little Billy's artwork on a cover. Think again. Look through some of the self-published books out there and you'll find a few. Some of the artists are better than others, but the work of Little Billy is obvious.

Now, it could be that you are convinced that your Little Billy is better than all the rest and nothing I can say will convince you not to use his artwork. It could also be that you are indeed trapped and though you don't really want to use Little Billy's artwork, you are going to use it to keep peace in the family. If that's the case, what you want to know is how to use his artwork.

The first thing you will have to do is get Little Billy's artwork into a digital format us-

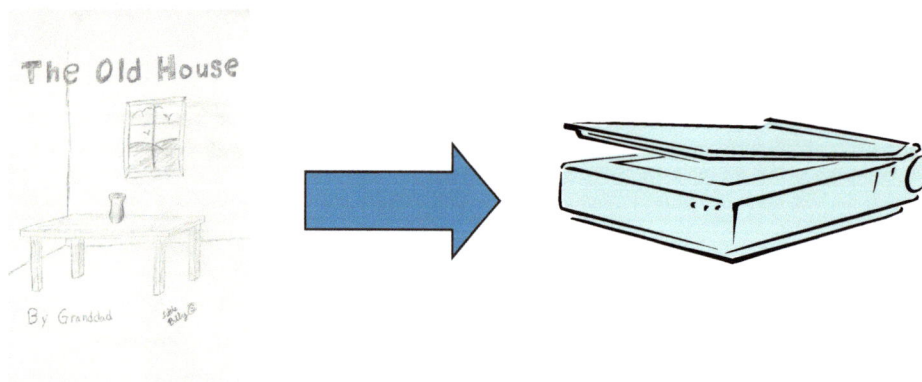

ing a scanner. If you don't have a scanner, you probably have a friend who does or you can take the drawing to a place like Fed-Ex Office that will let you borrow computer equipment for a fee. Scan the image in full color at 600 dpi, even if the drawing is in graphite. Though it may not look like there is color in the image, a color scan will be a more accurate representation of the image. The reason for scanning at 600 dpi is so that we can scale the image to fit our template. If we're already at 300 dpi and the image happens to be even a little too small, scaling the image to fit may cause pixelation.

After you've scanned in the image, open the template in Gimp and drag Little Billy's picture into the drawing area to create a new layer. As you can see from this example, the picture is too large for our template. To correct this, take the two measurement, using the Measure Tool , as is shown by the blue line and the light red line. The blue line is measuring the width of the front cover, the light red line is measuring the area of Little Billy's picture that we want to appear on the front cover. Divide the blue line distance by the light red line distance and multiple by 100 to give you a percentage. For the picture I used, I came up with an answer of 47%.

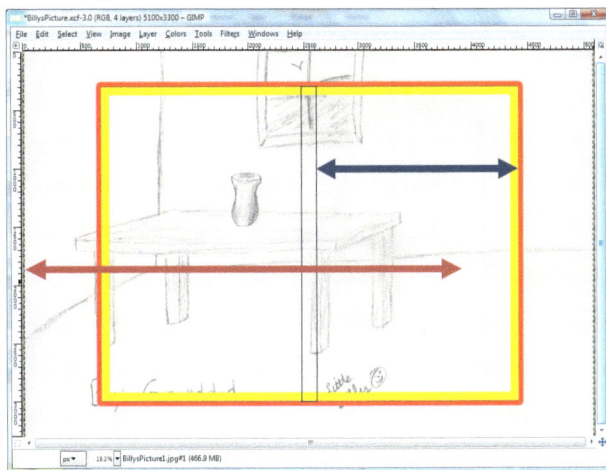

Select Layer|Scale Layer from the menus and enter the percentage. Click scale and Little Billy's picture will be the right size, you need only move it into position.

To complete the cover, you need only apply the techniques we've used with the other covers in this book. You can trim away part of the drawing that is spilling over into the spine using a Layer Mask. You can add a layer behind the drawing to set the color of the back cover. You can add text to the spine and the back cover.

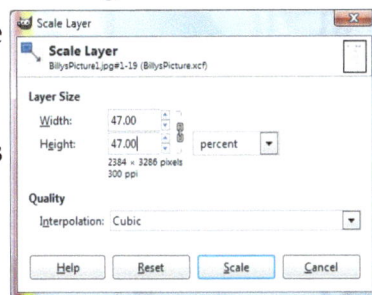

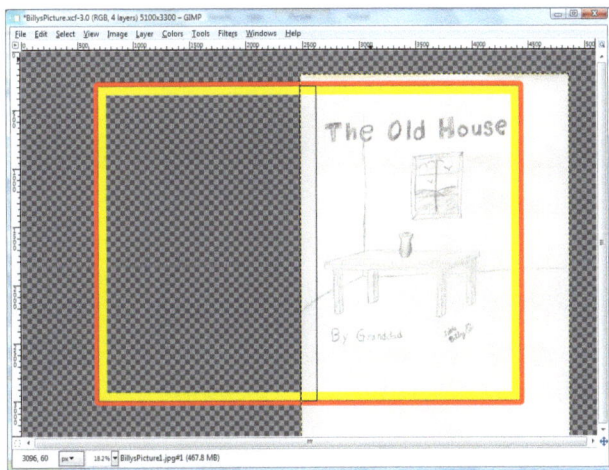

If you are really daring, you can use the Clone Tool to remove the lettering on the image and you can use the text tool to add a better looking title and the correct author's name.

But suppose it isn't as important that Little Billy's pencil drawing appear exactly as he drew it as it does that the images he drew appear on the cover. That opens the door of opportunity for us to improve upon his idea. Using Inkscape, we can produce a drawing that is similar to his, but one that will appear better in print.

Compare these images. Notice the increase in contrast from one to the other. It is almost as if someone took a black pen and traced the image. Actually, it is even better. All of those black lines in the new image are part of an Inkscape object. Just like all Inkscape objects, you can edit them. With almost no effort at all, you can remover the title and the author's name from the image. You can also resize the image without much thought to resolution.

To accomplish this, we need a lower resolution picture than the one we scanned in. The 600 dpi image is so large that Inkscape will choke on it, so use Gimp to scale the image to a 600x900 pixel image. Be sure to save it under a different name, because you may need the large image later. Drag the 600x900 pix-

86

el image into Inkscape. With the image selected, press Ctrl+Alt+B or select Path|Trace Bitmap from the menus. This will bring up the Trace Bitmap dialog.

You will need to play with the Threshold values and press the Update button to update the Preview until you see something similar to what you see here. For a pencil drawing, the brightness cutoff will work well. When you click Ok, Inkscape will cover Little Billy's drawing with a tracing of the image.

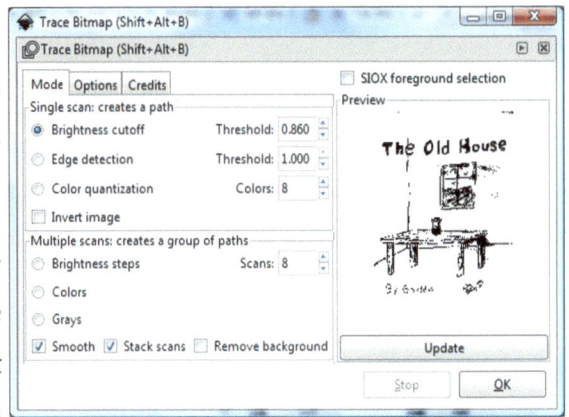

Before we move on, lets look at another reason why you might want to use this feature in Inkscape. Suppose you've gone to lunch with a buddy and on the back of a paper placemat you drew what you believe is a great logo for your widget manufacturing company, the best selling widget you have. But a drawing on a napkin isn't very useful as a logo. You scan it in and that gives you the image you see on the left, but if you're going to put it on everything from ink pens to coffee mugs, you'll need an image that will scale well. Once Inkscape traces the image for you, you can save the tracing as an .emf or .wmf file. With a file like that, scaling will be crystal clear in any program you use it in.

Or for a more realistic scenario, you need a logo to stick on the spine of a book. You either drew one by hand, or someone handed you a piece of paper with the logo on it. Depending on how the cover will be used, you may be working with someone else's logo, or you may be working with your own. If you are given a logo, you may still want to convert it into vector graphics. If you are working with your own logo, you most definitely want a vector graphics version of it so that you have more control over the image when you place it in the various places it is used. You may be using it in more places than just the spine and back cover if you are also responsible for designing the interior of the book.

There are also other types of objects that work better with vector graphics. If you have an image that appears often in a book you may want a vector graphics image that works like clipart.

But that still leaves us with Little Billy's picture. One of the things you can do with Little Billy's picture is to highlight the fact that it is a pencil drawing where another method would normally be used. Take a look at the image below.

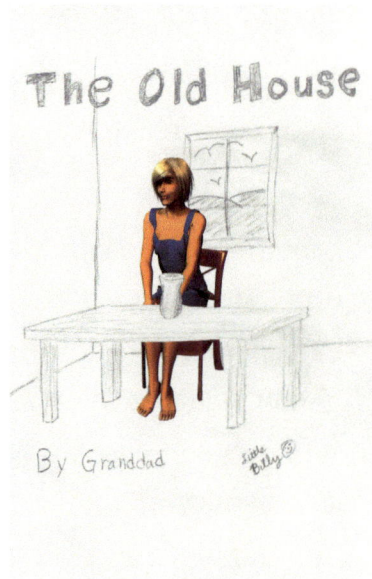

By combining two drawing methods that don't seem like they should work well together, we are actually drawing attention to their differences, but because we have put the spotlight on it, it looks like this is what we intended. It is very much like seeing someone on television interacting with cartoon characters. This method won't work with every book, but there are a few books for which it will.

Another method you can use that is similar is to include Little Billy's picture in another picture. For example, the cover of your romance novel might be a picture of a dress, like what we looked at earlier, but there might be a picture frame in the background that holds Little Billy's picture.

Little Billy's pictures are almost always troublesome and should be avoided, but with some creativity, you can find ways to make use of Little Billy's talent without making the cover of the book look worse than it must.

3D Graphics and Cover Design

While the primary focus of this book has been on two dimensional graphics, sections of it have relied heavily on three dimensional graphics. Glance through the offerings of self-publishers and small presses and what you'll find is extensive use of 3D graphics. You may find this more with science fiction and fantasy publishers than other publishers, but it is with good reason. Most of us don't own a spaceship that we can photograph as it makes its way around the sun. And most of us don't have friends who are willing to have gills surgically added just so we can take a picture.

You'll find that 3D graphics are used with other books because it is cheaper than paying the fees for stock photos or paying a model for a photo shoot. While I was writing this book, I made use of 3D graphics because of the convenience of it. So while I've avoided the discussion of 3D graphics so far because it requires a bit more skill than most of the people reading this book have and may require software that is too expensive to purchase just to do one cover, it is a topic that we shouldn't avoid.

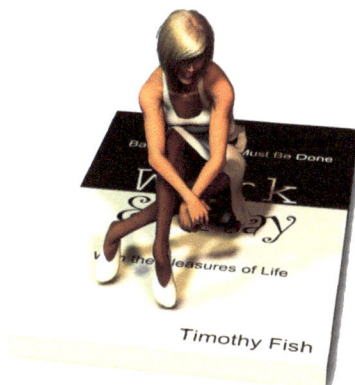

If you're looking for an easy and cheap way to get into 3D graphics, the place to start is with Art of Illusion (http://www.artofillusion.org). The software is free, it has a very intuitive user interface and a high quality render engine, but don't expect to use it to render people. While it is capable of doing that, there are other tools that are better for rendering people.

Once you begin looking at using 3D software, one of the things you will quickly discover is that there isn't just one tool that does everything well. Every tool has something that it does well, but then you have to rely on something else to complete the journey. So, I'm not going to even try to tell you how to use these tools. Instead, I want to focus on the output of these tools and how you can use that output for your covers. I don't want to tell you how to use the interface of your tool of choice, but rather focus on the things that are common to many tools.

Below is a character that was rendered with a 3D graphics program. Let's look at some of the telltale signs.

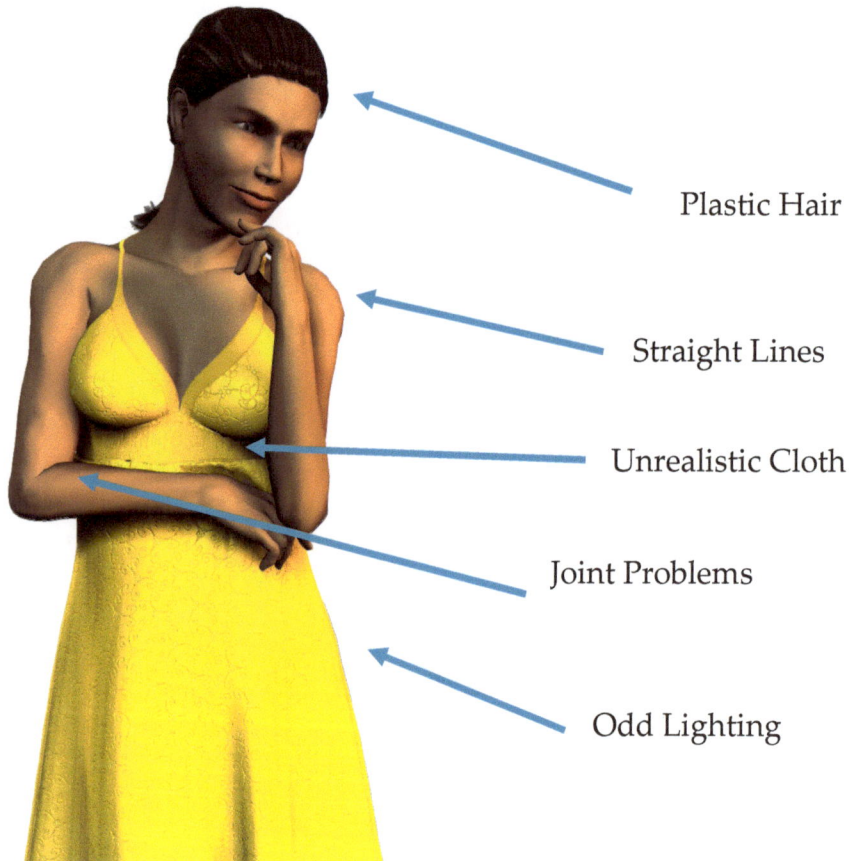

Plastic Hair

Straight Lines

Unrealistic Cloth

Joint Problems

Odd Lighting

While 3D rendering software has reached such a level of sophistication that it is possible to render images that almost impossible to distinguish from photographs of real people, it isn't always easy to accomplish and there are plenty of places that we can make mistakes. One such place is the hair. Some software packages include hair simulation. Autodesk Maya, which is something of the gold standard in 3D software and retails at about $3,500 obviously does, but common folk like us are more likely to use something like Smith Micro Poser, which is more in the $250 to $500 price range and is primarily focused on rendering people and characters. We're also more likely to be trying to run the software on a laptop than on a high powered workstation that produces enough heat to warm our house. Because of our limited capability, we'll skimp on the hair, either reducing the number of hairs on the head or we'll use something that looks like hair, but is actually just a scull cap that is streaked like hair might look. As you look at this woman's head, notice how the hair all begins its growth along a nice smooth curve at the top of her forehead. You can also see that the streaks are a little thick and not a hair is out of place. We expect hair to be somewhat shiny and to reflect light, but in this case it makes her look like she has layers of plastic on her head.

Compare the hair on the woman you see above with that of this next woman. Both women are posed in exactly the same way. But notice how this next woman's hair looks so much more like hair. It has some randomness to it. Sure, it has it's problems too and experienced 3D artists will spot it right away, but it is a big improvement. It doesn't look like it all grew from the same place because it didn't. The shininess of the hair looks like hair ought to look. If you're looking for things, there are plenty of things to spot, but it's good enough that if we mix it with some other things and adjust the lighting, it will look like it is supposed to be a real person and not a Barbie Doll.

The next issue I mentioned is that of straight lines showing up in odd places, such as on the woman's shoulder. But as you can see, there are ways to correct that as well. In this case, all we needed to do was to select a checkbox that told the software to smooth the polygons and re-render the image. You may find it helpful to understand why this problem exists and what we did by clicking the checkbox. Rather than looking at a woman's shoulder for our answer, it will be helpful if we turn to another object we expect to be smooth, a ball.

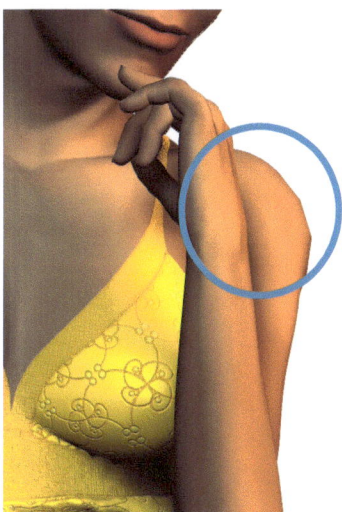

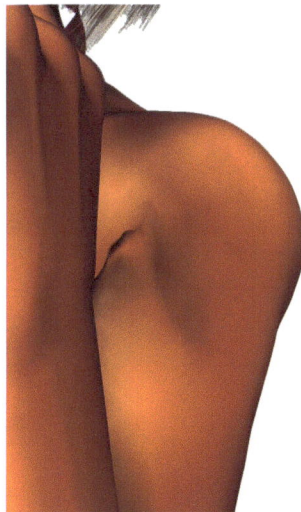

In this first image, you can see the unsmoothed ball. The interior of the ball looks nice and smooth, but when we see the same problem that we saw with the woman's shoulder. There are straight lines where it ought to be curved. This problem exists because the ball is represented in the software as a set of polygons. Polygons work well with 3D graphics because they are perfectly flat and a ray will intersect a triangle in one place. It simplifies the calculations and there are a lot of calculations when working with computer graphics.

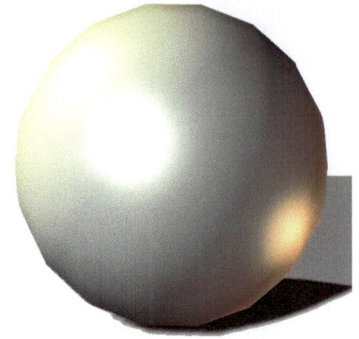

If you look at this next image you can see how the ball would look if we were to draw

it without the smooth shading. If you look at the edge of the ball, you can see that the straight lines there align with the lines we saw in the first drawing. This next drawing may show that even better. Here we have allowed the software to smooth the ball like normal, but we've drawn lines along the edges of the polygons. Along the edge, those lines match up with the corners we saw before.

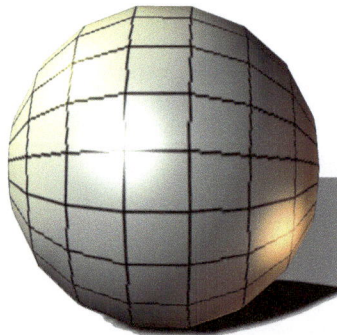

The next thing to look at is how the ball looks with the lines and with smoothing turned on.

In comparison to the other images, it looks like we've done something to make the ball rounder. In fact, we have. We used shading in the other images to give it a round look. The computer calculates the shade of each pixel in the polygon based on where the intersections of the lines are, but along the edges of the ball the polygons don't extend out far enough. The shading stops where the polygons stop. By turning the smoothing on, we've told the computer to draw outside the lines of the polygons. It takes more processing time because the computer has to determine where it should draw, but it makes the object appear nice and round. When we drew the woman's shoulder, the computer did the exact same thing.

The next thing on our list of problems is unrealistic cloth. This problem isn't as easy to fix. Notice in the image that the cloth simulation has bunched up the woman's dress above her arm. It's unlikely you would see something like this in real life and it is certainly unattractive on a book cover. There are a couple of things we can do about this. The easiest thing to do is to use Gimp to correct the image. We aren't doing animation, so all we really need is one good image.

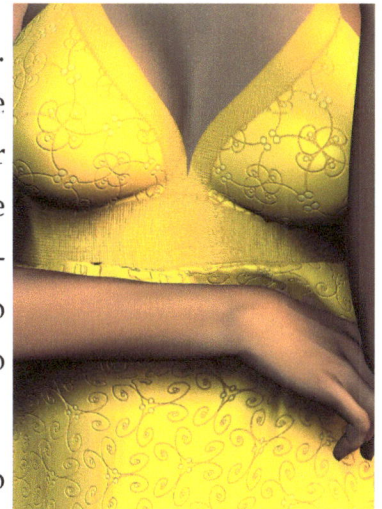

It requires more effort, but the correct way to fix this is to adjust the woman's pose so that it doesn't bunch up the material during the simulation. With a cloth simulation, we have some kind of starting pose and an ending pose. As the character moves from one pose to the next, the cloth folds to match the new position. If the model makes a motion that a real person wouldn't, that motion may catch the cloth object in some way that makes it behave in an odd way. To correct the problem, we have to edit the poses the model moves through so that body parts don't catch the cloth in the wrong way. Once that is done, the cloth should fall in to place properly.

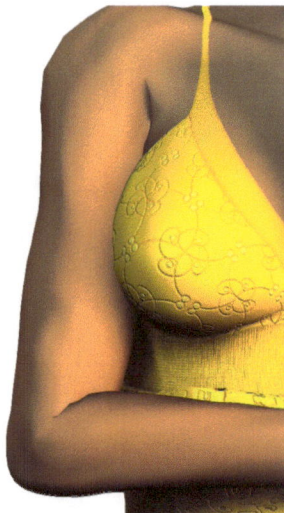

The joints on the model can also be a giveaway that the person is computer generated rather than real. 3D models are just skin and bones. The skin gives them their color. The bones determine their pose. Since they don't have meat on their bones, the skin may not bend the way it should. It may fold a little too tightly in some places and too loosely in others. Polygon smoothing helps, but it doesn't always fix the problem. That's where Gimp comes into play. Once we've gotten am image that is close to what we want with the 3D tool, we can use Gimp and the Smudge tool or one of the other tools to help us fix the problems and make the image look even better.

The last thing I mentioned was lighting. Lighting can either help you or hurt you when it comes to 3D graphics. Darker lighting, for example, often helps to sell the 3D model as a real person because it helps to hide the flaws. But if you look at this image you can see that there is a gray shadow back there. That's not to say that such a shadow couldn't exist, but we normally don't have a perfectly flat white surface for a shadow to fall on in real life. This causes the image to stand out as fake.

But we can fix it by including more realistic backgrounds and by adjusting the lighting so that it looks more natural.

Unless you are designing covers for speculative fiction, perhaps one of the biggest arguments against using 3D software to generate people for your covers is the clothing, or the lack thereof.

It isn't that you can't find clothing. There are artists who are generating 3D content for sale all the time, but much of it is quite skimpy or it looks something like this:

Next time you design a cover for the latest Amish romance novel , put that guy on the front and see how well it goes over. But someone went to a lot of trouble to design all of that stuff our guy is wearing. Unless you can find the right clothes for your models among all of the science fiction, fantasy and pornographic offerings, you'll have to design it yourself. That process can be as troublesome as learning to do all of the stuff we've looked at in this book. Not only do you need to know how to handle tools like Gimp, you'll need to know how to create and edit the 3D meshes and objects that form the characters' clothes. That is well beyond the scope of this book. But 3D graphics can give us the ability to bring nearly any character into photo realistic being.

Let's Do Better

We've reached the end of our little journey and I hope that something I have said will encourage you to try your hand at producing better book covers. More than a million books are published each year and about half of those have covers that could have been designed by people like us, the common folk. There is no way to foresee everything that you might need in producing a cover, but you should have enough tools to get you start-

ed. More and more books are being self-published or published by small presses, so more and more people just like us will have the opportunity to produce covers for those books. We need something better than the hastily generated covers that are nothing more than generic images with text. Let's make use of the tools we have available to us and produce better covers that not only make our books look better but better represent their content.

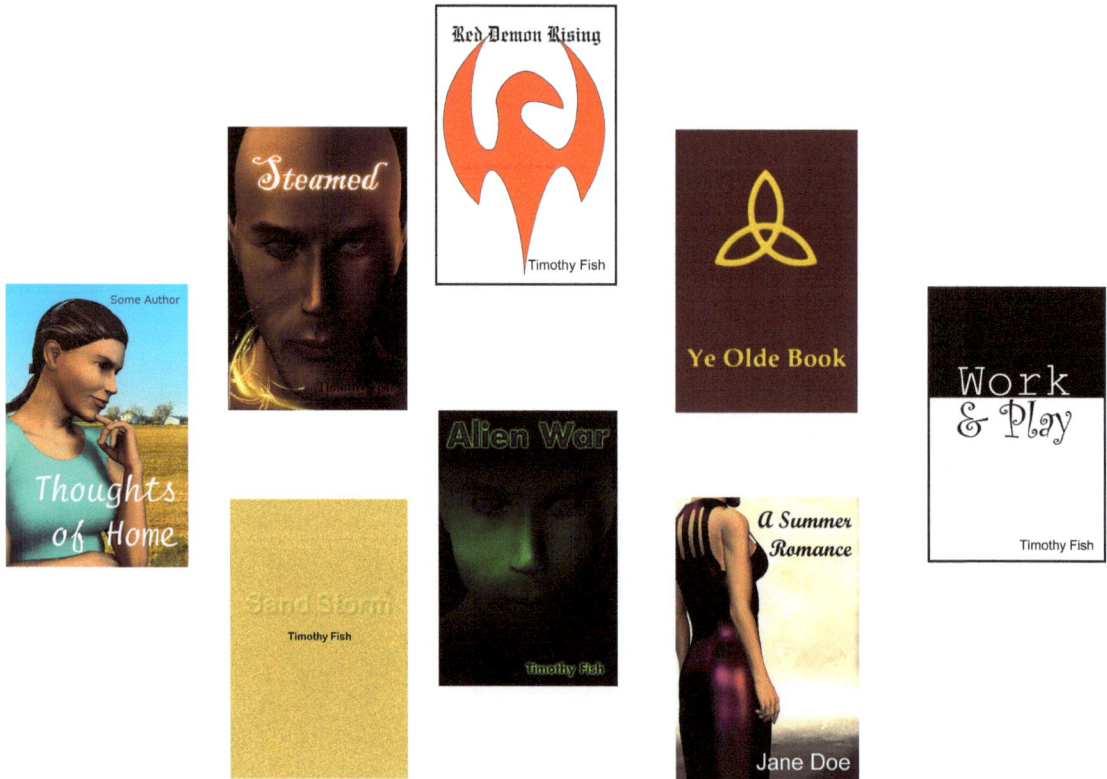

About The Author:

Timothy has been involved with publishing for most of his life. In his younger years he became quite adept at folding newsletters and holding the string with his finger while his father tied bundles of associational minute books. He is the author of seven books, not counting the one he authored in kindergarten and is the publisher of eleven books.

Timothy maintains a blog at http://timothyfish.blogspot.com where he primarily discusses topics related to publishing and writing.

Also From the Author

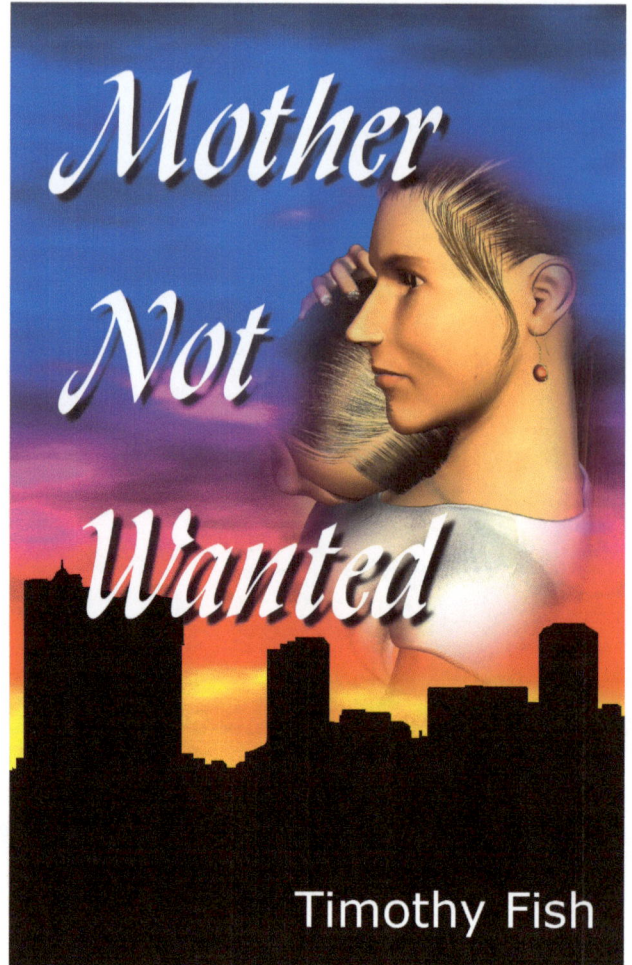

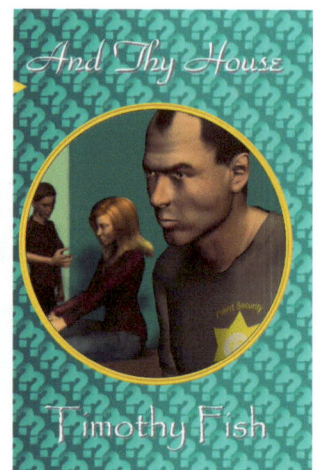

Church Website Design
A Step By Step Approach

Timothy Fish

Mother Not Wanted

Timothy Fish

Searching For Mom

Timothy Fish

How To Become A Bible Character

Timothy Fish

For the Love of a Devil

Timothy Fish

And Thy House

Timothy Fish

www.ingramcontent.com/pod-product-compliance
Lightning Source LLC
Chambersburg PA
CBHW060805270326
41927CB00002B/52